KU-506-851

Discover
Rewarding
Photography

Discover Rewarding Photography

by Ronald Spillman A.I.I.P.

THE MANUAL OF RUSSIAN EQUIPMENT

First published in Great Britain in 1971
by Technical & Optical Equipment (London) Ltd
Zenith House, Thane Villas, London N.7.

Copyright © 1971 by Technical & Optical Equipment
All rights reserved.

SBN 9502072 0 9

Designed & Produced by
Don Cheesman & Associates, Beckenham,
Kent.

Printed & bound by
Sir Joseph Causton & Sons Ltd., London
and Eastleigh.

Contents

A message . . . .

The purpose of this book is that after having purchased one of our cameras we want to ensure that you obtain the maximum benefit by introducing you to the fascinating world of photography that can be yours with very little study, and to this end, we have asked Mr. Ronald Spillman, an acknowledged expert on this subject, to convey to you some of the benefits of his vast knowledge in an easily readable form.

For many of us there are certain fleeting moments of life that once experienced are gone for ever, but with photography these special moments can be captured and relived; a growing child, a memorable holiday, a golden sunset, or the living world in miniature that abounds around us, even in our own back garden, which close-up photography can reveal.

I, together with all of my colleagues at Technical & Optical, hope that this book will increase your understanding of photography and in many ways enhance your interest in life itself.

J. N. HAPGOOD,
Managing Director.

Introduction

Here at the beginning, may I draw your attention to the meaning of our title—*Discover Rewarding Photography*. Those three words were chosen very carefully to describe what this manual has in store for you.

In the first place, I would like you to come on a voyage of discovery with me, into the world of photography that already interests you. You see, I want you to discover more, learn more, about photography. It is a well-known fact that what we get out of life depends largely on what we are prepared to put into it.

The second word of our title, rewarding, describes the kind of photography I want to put before you. Properly approached, this fascinating hobby offers tremendous rewards. It is an outlet for whatever creative talents we possess and, in another direction, gives us endless satisfaction when our pictures of people, events, family occasions are admired and give joy to others.

And the third word is photography itself. Think of this manual as a short course designed to bring you to better technique and picture appreciation. I shall be at your elbow guiding you along the way.

Ron Spillman

This is Photography

We need three things in order to develop from the snapshot stage to a mature, creative ability with a camera. First, we must develop our feeling for aesthetics, the appreciation of line and form, of colour, of balance and the dynamic, so that the images we put on film may speak with beauty. Second, we must deepen our knowledge of the technical side of our medium, so that camera and film will produce for us the images we wish to capture for others to see. Third, just as the painter has more than one brush, we will eventually feel the need for another lens perhaps, or some filters, to broaden our scope.

Part I: Aesthetic

Photography's subjects are as wide as those of life itself and a catalogue of them is a description of living. Take such branches as pictorial, portrait, wedding, glamour, abstract, record, architecture, fashion and holiday. It's really like describing life, isn't it, with something for everyone.
Let's look at these subjects one by one, so that we can make the most of those that interest us.

Pictorial

The word pictorial is used exclusively by camera clubs and those with similar views, to describe a club idea of a photograph with artistic merit. The word is never used in this sense by painters or sculptors, and you may decide that this is significant. The carefully composed picture of a piper on a russet hillside with distant tarn and clouds, is a pictorial view. The description for many years fitted endlessly similar amateur exhibitions and salons of photography. Walls were lined with visual clichés, a wagon wheel leaning against a farm wall, a painstakingly-lit character study of an old man with beard, a self-conscious girl-friend trying to look soulful with a shawl over her head.

Today the field of pictorialism opens out as young blood infiltrates the diehards at many clubs. Pictures of real people doing real things are now commonplace, and details of landscape, revelations of texture, are taking precedence over the formal S-curve of pathway 'leading' the eye gently back to the windmill at the focal point on the horizon. Even a calm sunset, shading gold with sun's embers, can affect the viewer mightily. So here, I suggest, is a set of 'rules' of composition for today's photographer.

(1) Do most of the composition in the viewfinder. Don't rely on the enlarger.
(2) The shape of your finished picture should be pre-visualised, to suit the subject. Square frames are more static than oblong ones.
(3) We want balance, not symmetry. Objects of uneven

size balancing each other, rather than geometric arrangement of objects of equal size.

(4) For impact, isolate your subject from fussy backgrounds and fill the frame with it. If something doesn't actively help the picture, eliminate it.

(5) Vertical subjects and picture shapes are more dynamic than horizontal ones. Centre placings are static; oblique placings are dynamic.

(6) Keep it simple. A few bold, contrasting masses balancing each other is the golden rule.

(7) Arrange the size of the main subject in relation to the frame to suggest smallness or greatness. A child's smallness is suggested by having some space round it; a young woman can share the frame with the background; a strong character head can fill the frame.

(8) A high viewpoint suggests the smallness of the subject, insignificance, or fear. A low viewpoint suggests the height of the subject, importance, or the heroic. Relate your photographic viewpoint to the obvious psychological inferences. Looking 'up to' or 'down on' someone.

(9) With colour, complimentary colours suggest harmony, clashing colours suggest conflict.

(10) One small area of bright colour gives accent to a large pastel area, e.g. a poppy in a cornfield.

(11) The eye is selective, the camera isn't, so don't photograph a riot of variegated flowers. See Figs. 87 and 88. Fruit salad is better in a bowl than on colour film.

(12) All rules are meant to be broken—they are only guide lines. Some of the factors that make a successful composition obviously apply to all branches of photography.

Portrait

A portrait isn't just a map of a face. If it were, we might just as well photograph a dummy or a mask. Rather, a successful portrait should reveal a major aspect of the sitter's personality. See Fig. 3. The trick is to draw the

Fig. 1. This is a happy event, so big smiles are more natural than stiff, posed expressions. Weddings cannot be repeated, so 'bridge' your exposures, giving some half a stop more, some half a stop less, plus normal. Ektachrome film.

Fig. 2. A typical pictorial view, full of open-air atmosphere. The piper has obviously been posed, but this kind of picture pleases a great many people. Ektachrome film.

sitter out, getting him or her to respond in characteristic vein capturing the expression at the psychological moment.

It's much harder to do this with formal studio lighting. If the sitter has to hold still at a certain angle, not daring to move because a carefully arranged nose shadow might reach the lips, then you aren't going to get natural portraits. Here are your guide lines for successful portraits that will make people gasp: 'That's him (or her) to a T!'

(1) Don't fumble with equipment. You may love it, but all the sitter is interested in is the end result. Have everything ready and the exposure set before you ask the sitter to do anything.

(2) Don't shine bright lights in the sitter's eyes. Diffused or reflected lighting is best. Where shadows are soft and without sharp edges, it doesn't matter if the sitter turns his head.

(3) Have light strong enough to allow hand-held, expression-stopping exposures, without having to ask the sitter to 'hold it'. Two photofloods without reflectors and fast film will allow 1/125th second at f/5.6.

(4) Sit and talk to your sitter, with the camera at your eye. Find out what she or he is interested in, express an interest and ask questions. Take pictures while the eyes light up and the answers come thick and fast.

(5) Occasionally, you may ask for a turn or a tilt of the head, but move yourself rather than the sitter.

(6) Don't amputate legs at the ankle, arms at the wrist. Stick to head-and-shoulders, half-length (with both arms included), full seated, kneeling or standing figures (again, with all limbs intact).

Weddings

A glance in the window of any good professional wedding photographer will show the formal aspects of the subject. Better still, a good professional album. The best wedding photographs include 'informals' such as cutting the cake, opening the dance, speeches and telegrams, and so on to the going away picture, complete with old boot (old white cricket boots show up best). Every bride wants formal pictures first. In front of the church you pose bride first, half then full-length; bride and groom, half (see Fig. 1) and full-length; then add bridesmaids and page; then add parents, his on her side, hers on his; then add family and friends—meanwhile changing to a wide-angle lens if you can't get back far enough.

Beforehand, take: half-length of best man adjusting groom's tie or buttonhole; various arrivals, especially bride being helped from car; bride coming up path on father's arm (see Fig. 104).

Afterwards, take: bride and groom smiling inwards over shoulders at camera as they go down path; confetti; couple in car (usually with flash through open car door).

With black and white film aim for a soft negative that will reproduce detail in groom's suit and bride's dress, about which she'll be as concerned as for her face. If the sun is casting harsh shadows and the surroundings allow, pose groups with backs turned three-quarters to the sun. Some professionals fill-in harsh shadows and reduce contrast in both black and white and colour by using flash in combination with the daylight exposure.

Glamour

Apart from news photographs, the world's press uses more pictures of pretty girls than any other subject. After all, they do make the world go round. Have a look at Figs. 4, 84, 85, 93, 99, 109, 115. What they have in common provides your guide to tasteful glamour photography.

(1) Go for natural, rather than artificial poses.

(2) Let the expression be frank and smiling or pensive, but *never* inviting.

(3) Good grooming and unobtrusive make-up are of great importance.

(4) No photographer or model need feel ashamed or self-conscious about revealing a certain amount of a pretty girl's natural attributes, but it must be done naturally. The dedicated photographer has no time for the immature, crude or suggestive pose.

(5) Minimise your model's less good points. Projecting

knee-cap, have leg bent gracefully. Thick waist, use elastic belt over or under dress, pin dress at back. Longish nose or small chin, low angle. Close-set eyes, try semi-profile. Remove bra straps half hour before taking pictures, if shoulders are to be shown bare.

(6) If taking glamour pictures for sale, study the various markets first.

Abstract

What is an abstract? We could apply several artistic definitions. A subject treated in such a way that it achieves its appeal to the viewer emotionally, without the distracting influence of recognizable objects, is about as close as we can come. All kinds of familiar objects lend themselves to the photography of attractive abstracts.

How about: reflections in water (see Fig. 5), paint on a palette, details of yarn or rope, patterns in crumbling plaster or old walls, sections of ironwork, reflections of coloured papers in crumpled silver paper, sections of railway line, a sleeper back-lit by low sun, melon seeds or a section through a cabbage?

Contrast is often a help when making abstracts in black and white, as it helps to eliminate all the half tones we associate with normal viewing. Easiest way to achieve this is to develop for a normal negative (you may want normal prints from other negatives on the same roll) then print on the most contrasty glossy paper, grade 5 or 6. The technique will be more fully described in the chapter on enlarging.

Record

We may want to make a record of anything from a postage stamp to the yearly height of a sapling. The great thing about record photography is that fine detail takes precedence over aesthetic considerations, though the two often go hand in hand. Slow and medium speed films are best for this

Fig. 3. On overseas holidays everyone wants to take character studies like this. Offer a friendly smile first, then show the camera. If you receive an affirmative nod, you can start shooting. *But smile.* Agfachrome.

purpose and a certain amount of ancillary equipment may be necessary.

(1) When copying flat subjects such as leaves from a book, the camera must be exactly parallel to, and on axis with, the centre of the subject. A good way is to screw the camera to an arm which fits the column of the enlarger. The matter to be copied is laid flat on the baseboard, with a heavy sheet of glass over, in the case of an open book. The camera can then be raised or lowered as desired.

(2) At least two lamps should be used, one at each side, at an angle not steeper than 45° to the flat matter. This will avoid reflections back into the camera lens.

(3) Normal reflected light exposure readings are all right for most half tone matter. In the case of black type on white paper, or other line work, lay a sheet of mid-grey or brown wrapping paper over the work and take a reading from that.

(4) For colour copying, use daylight type colour film, substituting electronic flash or blue flashbulbs for the lamps. Or use daylight (see Fig. 6). Or use artificial light type film by tungsten light, with a suitable filter if necessary.

(5) When photographing subjects *in situ*, architectural details, etc., always use a good tripod. Even if the light is bright enough for hand-held exposures, the tripod lets you pay close attention to viewpoint and exact framing. It also ensures optimum sharpness on enlargement.

(6) To get a good black and white print from a copy negative of a line subject, enlarge on high contrast bromide paper, giving *just enough* enlarging exposure to ensure a good black line. Couple this with full paper development.

Fig. 4. The best glamour is shot outdoors. Even professional studio work is nowadays considered old hat. A well-groomed model and carefully selected location outdoors are the elements of success.

Fig. 5. Sometimes, just a detail of a scene says as much as the whole. Abstract pictures speak direct to the emotions, without much interference from recognizable objects.

Fig. 6. Record photography calls for precise technique, as its prime object is to reveal every detail of the subject. Whenever possible, use a solid tripod or firm support and stop the lens down two or three stops for optimum performance.

Fig. 7. The small camera user does not have technical movements to keep verticals from converging. But he can achieve the same result by using a wide-angle lens. Agfacolor film.

Fig. 8. Fashion photography is a specialised field calling for great flair. Here, even the expert relies on an experienced model who can project the clothes rather than herself. Ektachrome film.

Architecture

The professional architectural photographer uses a stand camera with rising and falling front and swing-and-tilt movements, as architectural magazines demand that all verticals should be parallel. An ordinary camera does not have a rising front and if we tilt it up to include the top of a tall building the verticals will converge.

One way round this is to use a wide-angle lens. This will include more than the standard lens from a given distance, and it will often be possible to include the top of even the tallest building without tilting the camera upwards. Of course, only a portion of a negative or slide will contain the subject, but this area can be enlarged later. See Fig. 7.

Most amateurs and professionals are interested in architecture more from the historic point of view and cameras such as the Zenith-E or Zenith-80, especially when equipped with a wide-angle, and perhaps a telephoto lens to bring close details beyond reach of a normal lens, are ideal.

Fashion outdoors

Fashion is a highly specialised subject. Either you have a flair for it, or you haven't. Not all fashion photographers are called upon to reach the esoteric heights of the few magazines like *Vogue*. For every one of these, fifty thousand more down-to-earth ones are taken for catalogues, mail order brochures, knitting leaflets, dress pattern envelopes, and fashion store display. The secret of good fashion photography, and what differentiates it from glamour, is that it is designed to sell the clothes, not the girl. The good fashion model knows this, and poses accordingly. It also explains why the beanpole model of Haute Couture so often wears a haughty, unapproachable expression. You aren't supposed to be interested in her as a person.

An interesting technical aspect of fashion photography, is that the 6 × 6cm single-lens reflex, like the Zenith-80, has become almost the status symbol, or badge of office for the photographer.

When modelling outdoor clothes, especially those of a casual nature, the model is allowed to become quite human. She must appear to be enjoying wearing her outfit, but without projecting her personality at the camera. See Fig. 8. A famous fashion photographer once said 'In this game you need the camera, someone to load it for you, an experienced model, and no rheumatism in your trigger finger'.

Holidays

Nowadays, everyone can do better than those stand-up, grinning portraits on the beach, which look like the 1890's in modern beachwear. Good portraiture on holiday is the same as good portraiture elsewhere, but on holiday we often want to show our companions in relation to the setting. We all know the old funny about the photographer walking

Fig. 9. The elements of success in a fine holiday shot. Attractive couple, clear background, good colour, sun with flash to lighten the shadows, and super action. Ektachrome film.

Fig. 10. By moving the camera
with the car, the photographer
rendered the car sharply, but
the background slightly blurred
to help the impression of speed.
Tilting the camera gives a
dynamic, diagonal direction.

backwards on a mountain ledge while composing his fellow-
climber against the Matterhorn. They reached him next day,
but the camera was unhurt.

Instead of walking backwards, whether on mountain
ledges or in front of Nelson's Column, simply change to
your wide-angle lens. This allows you to get close to your
companion, so that he or she is in the foreground of your
picture, but the angle of acceptance of the wide-angle lens is
such that all the background can be included too. Leisure
and action go well together, as in Fig. 9.

When travelling abroad, make sure you have enough film
with you, as your favourite brand may be unobtainable or
very expensive. If you want to take a large supply of film
with you, ask your travel agent for the Customs regulations
regarding import of film in the countries you are visiting.
When travelling in hot countries by car, never keep film
(especially colour film) in the glove compartment or near the
engine. It will be badly affected.

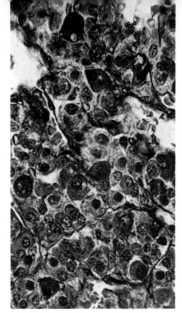

Fig. 11. Clinical slides made with a Zenith–E mounted on a Russian microscope, give the doctor and the scientist vital information. This equipment also opens up a colourful, abstract world to the amateur.

Fig. 12. 35mm single-lens reflexes such as the Zenith-E cope swiftly with everything from helicopter rescue to baby shows. Depth of field and handling facility are the key words. Kodachrome film.

A long telephoto, of 200mm or even 300mm is invaluable when taking candid pictures of colourful characters abroad. Far better than aiming a standard lens at their faces from a yard or so away. The longer Russian lenses handle well and steadily in the hand, and there is no finer outfit for candids, among other subjects, than the 300mm Zenith-E combination known as the Photo-Sniper.

To sum up, there are certain aspects of photography that apply to every field we have discussed. Good, clean technique is common to them all. So is good equipment. To make the most of any of the more specialist branches, a word of advice I cannot stress too much—study all the best work of the type, whether in specialist magazines, or other publications. Analyse each picture and try to determine how it was taken, with what kind of materials and equipment.

Part II: Technical

Let the sunshine in . . .

Look at a modern camera—for example, the Zenith-E—and it may be difficult to relate it to the old-fashioned box with which our ancestors were able to take snapshots. Yet the two share a common function. Each has a lens to project an image onto the film in the interior. Each has a device to allow the image to enter for the right amount of time.

The difference is one of scope, rather than function.

The basic concepts

Focusing, together with the selection of shutter speed and lens aperture produce the exposure and apart from experience, these three factors tell the whole story of successful photography. Let's examine them one at a time, then bring them together into an easy picture-taking technique.

Fig. 13. A box camera had a lens at one end to throw a picture of whatever was before it on to the film at the other end. As snaps were seldom enlarged, the quality of the image did not have to be high.

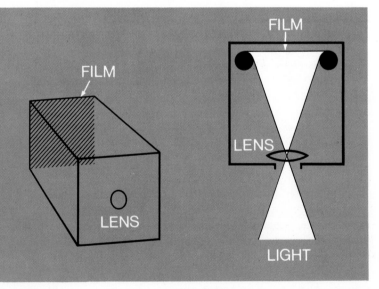

Focusing

Just as with binoculars, the lens has to be focused on the subject. Set the focusing ring at 10′ (Approx. 3m) and a subject at that distance from the camera will be sharply in focus. This point of focus is somewhat theoretical, because a certain distance on either side of it, towards and away from the camera, will also appear reasonably sharp. This total area of sharpness either side of the point of true focus is called the *depth of field*.

(1) Depth of field is greater the farther the point of focus from the camera.

(2) Depth of field is greater beyond the subject than in front of the subject.

(3) Depth of field is greater, the smaller the lens aperture.

(4) Conversely, depth of field is less, the larger the lens aperture. (see Fig. 15.)

On modern miniature cameras, lenses usually have a maximum aperture of f/2 or f2.8, though certain lenses for

Fig. 14. A superb single-lens reflex like the Zenith does exactly the same job as the simple box—it projects a light image on film. But it does this far more accurately, with greater facility and with infinitely more scope.

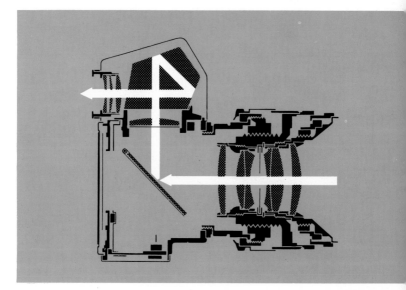

high speed work go up to f/1.4. Fig. 16 demonstrates that each larger aperture transmits twice as much light as the previous one. This fact has a direct bearing on the subject of exposure, which will be examined shortly.

Film speed

The speed of the film or, to be more accurate, its degree of sensitivity to light, is often measured by an ASA rating, which can be found on the film carton. The various groups can be divided as follows:
SLOW (25–50 ASA); MEDIUM (64–125 ASA);
FAST (200–400 ASA); EXTRA FAST (800–3200 ASA).

What you need to know

(1) The slower the film, the finer the grain structure that will be visible on enlargement.
(2) The faster the film, the coarser the grain structure that will be visible on enlargement.

Fig. 15. Depth of field is the area of apparent sharpness extending either side of the point focused on. It increases as the lens aperture is made smaller, diminishes as the aperture is enlarged.

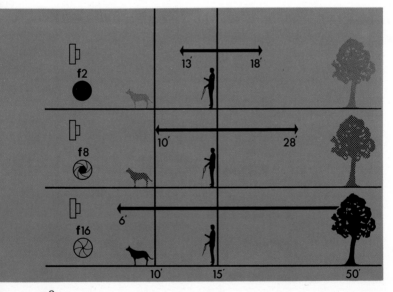

(3) With identical enlargements up to about 7″ × 5″, you'll see practically no granular difference between slow and faster films.

(4) Reserve the fast and extra fast films for action and poor light photography.

(5) A medium speed film will cope with most subjects and situations and, provided exposure and processing were correct, give big enlargements of high quality.

(6) Naturally, the faster the film the smaller the lens aperture you may use for a given shutter speed and subject brightness.

So you see, we now understand how a lens may be brought into sharp *focus* on a film of given *sensitivity*, and the depth of field controlled by the diaphragm.

Exposure determination

The lens aperture controls the brightness of the image falling on the film, the shutter controls the amount of time

Fig. 16. Each lens aperture, or stop, or f number, lets through twice as much light as the next smaller one, half as much light as the next larger one.

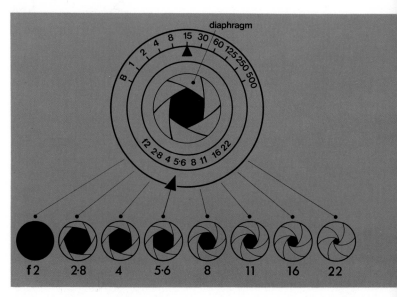

for which the image is allowed to affect the film. Let's put all the facts together in a practical demonstration. We have a scene of a certain brightness and a film of a certain sensitivity. Although faster, the film reacts to light the way our skin reacts to ultra-violet rays from the sun. Not enough exposure and we stay white, too much and we burn. In photographic terms, under-exposed and over-exposed. So how do we choose the correct combination of lens aperture and shutter speed, to give the film the right amount of exposure?

We measure the brightness of the scene by means of an exposure meter, either the built-in meter type or by means of a separate meter. As you can see in Figs. 17 and 18, there are two methods of using a separate meter, one by reflected light, the other by incident light. Using a little care, either method will give a satisfactory reading.

First set the meter for the ASA rating of the film in use. Point the meter at the subject in the case of reflected light

Fig. 17. Pointing at the subject, the reflected light meter measures the light reflected from the subject. Take the meter close to the subject if the surroundings or background are much darker or lighter than the subject.

use, or from the subject position towards the camera in the case of incident light use. The meter needle will indicate the brightness and the simple alignment with an index pointer gives you the correct exposure—*or does it!*

Suppose for a given film speed in a given lighting situation, the meter reading is like this:

shutter speed :	1000	500	250	125	60	30	15
lens aperture :	f/2	f/2.8	f/4	f/5.6	f/8	f/11	f/16

Any pair would give the same amount of exposure to the film, for example 1/500th second at f/2.8 or 1/30th second at f/11. The one thing the meter cannot tell us is which pair to choose, but our choice can be easily made by remembering a few general principles. If, to what we already know about lens apertures controlling the depth of field, we add the self-evident fact that faster shutter speeds control the action-stopping capability of the lens, we can decide for ourselves. A few examples will make this clear. We'll assume that in each case the meter reading is as above.

Fig. 18. The incident light meter is aimed from the subject position towards the camera, and measures the light falling on the subject. It always gives the correct reading for skin tones.

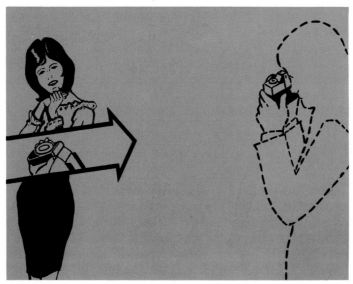

(1) *Half-length portrait :* Quite easy to decide, as the only action here takes place as the smile forms on the model's face. Possibly she'll wave a hand. That amount of movement will be taken care of by a shutter speed of 1/125th second, so we can give 1/125th at f/5.6.

(2) *Racing Car :* To stop the rapid action here, even when panning the camera to keep the car central in the viewfinder, we'll need 1/500th second, so we choose that shutter speed with the lens aperture f/2.8. We must focus carefully on a point we know the car will pass, as there is not much depth of field at f/2.8.

(3) *Village pump, distant cottages :* In order to keep sharpness on the close-by pump and the cottages, we need great depth of field, so we choose a small aperture, f/11, and set the shutter at 1/30th second. 1/30th was the shutter speed for which old-fashioned box cameras were nearly always set, and the camera needs to be held very steady at the moment of exposure, otherwise we'll get a blurred picture.

In the first two examples, both of moving subjects, the choice of shutter speed was of prime importance. So we chose a shutter speed sufficient to arrest the movement and relied on the meter to tell us what lens aperture to use at the selected speed.

In the third example, depth of field was important, so we selected a small lens aperture, setting the shutter speed accordingly.

Remember two things, however. All combinations of shutter speed and lens aperture are a compromise and there is really no 'correct' exposure for any subject. What is 'correct' at 1/500th second at f/5.6 will also be satisfactory at 1/250th at f/8 or 1/1000th second at f/4. Remember also that few people can hold a camera consistently steady at shutter speeds as slow as 1/30th second, and certainly not slower, though experienced pressmen get away with it time and again. When out and about on a summer's day with a medium speed film in the camera, a setting of 1/125th at f/16, with the lens focused at 15′ (Approx. 5m) will hardly ever need to be adjusted.

Single-Lens Reflex

The single-lens reflex has had more influence on photography in the years since its introduction, than any previous camera design. That exciting parallax-free screen, with its lens-eye-film faithfulness, plus the fact that you can capture reality a mere squeeze after it occurs, has raised the SLR to the pinnacle of popularity. Just as important, if not more so, is the creative influence on the photographer, as he absorbs visually through the screen the language of depth of field, differential focusing, significant relationships between objects and figures and the frame.

This chapter deals with the capability of the modern single-lens reflex, alone and as part of a system which widens its scope into every field of photography. We shall also discuss the way to choose lenses and accessories for our own particular purposes.

SLR

TURN BACK for a moment to what we said about the single-lens reflex. Remember? It does the same job as an old box camera, the lens at one end throws a light picture on to a film at the other end—only the SLR is far more sophisticated, and has infinitely more scope. Fine words, but what do they mean in terms of using the camera, and in the results it enables us to get?

Glance back at Fig. 14. It works this way. First, you look into the viewfinder eyepiece. What you see there is the same image that will fall on the film. You see it right way up, right way round, and, in the Zenith, you see it very bright. Assume you have now set the lens aperture and the shutter speed according to your meter reading, and you press the shutter release button. In a fraction of a second, several linked actions take place. The mirror flies up out of the path between lens and film plane. As it reaches top, it blocks off light filtering down through the pentaprism from the eyepiece. Instantly, the focal plane shutter begins its traverse and the film is exposed. Directly the shutter blinds finish this movement the mirror flies down again. It all happens so fast that you are simply aware of a 'blink'. Viewing, in fact, is virtually continuous.

Parallax-free viewing

When you look into the viewfinder of an ordinary camera, you must bear in mind that you are observing the scene from a different viewpoint to that of the lens. The viewfinder and lens may be a couple of inches apart. Looking at a distant scene, that two inches may be quite negligible, but in close-up photography, the difference can be serious.

The difference is know as *parallax error,* and accounts for all those heads we see chopped off on amateur portraits. To overcome this, some viewfinders have marks to indicate the top of the frame when working at close quarters. This merely makes you point the camera up a little, but it doesn't correct parallax. It merely compensates for it.

This is one of the great advantages of the single-lens reflex. There is no parallax error at all. The film will 'see' the picture as you did, from exactly the same angle. The fact gives tremendous confidence to the user and is, of course, invaluable when he begins to explore the fascinating world of close-up, and especially macro-photography.

Compositional aid

Equally important, is that the viewing system shows you the subject, plus the various planes before and behind it, the same way that the lens sees them. If you are using a wide aperture which, as we know, gives only shallow depth of field, you can observe the fact directly in the viewfinder screen. The subject will appear sharp, the nearer or more distant parts relatively less sharp.

This aids tremendously in creative photography, and is what we call *differential focusing*. The idea is that by having the subject stand out sharply against a purposely out-of-focus background, we give extra attention to it. Our picture gains impact.

Fig. 19. Leader among Russian SLR's is the Zenith-E with its excellent 58mm f/2 Helios lens. Shutter speeds to 1/500th second. Instant return mirror and efficient built-in exposure meter.

Fig. 20. Virtually identical with the Zenith-E, the Zenith-B has the same fine optics, shutter accuracy and other facilities, lacking only the built-in meter.

Fig. 21. This version of the Zenith-B has a very fine 50mm f/3.5 Industar lens. Less fast than the Helios, it is capable of resolving ultra fine detail.

Fig. 22. Taken in the park with a standard 50mm lens. The deer and trees make a nice pattern, but the deer would have wandered off if the camera had come too close. The Zenith is ideal for such work.

Other screen advantages

The SLR screen is also the finest way to learn how wide-angle and telephoto lenses behave, because we see the result right there on the screen. We learn how perspective fans out sharply from a powerful foreground when we screw in our wide-angle; we see the flattening of planes when the telephoto brings distant life unknowingly before us. We learn, in fact, how to use the qualities of a certain lens to present our picture in a certain way. The SLR user can use lenses in focal lengths up to 1000mm, in the shape of the handy, catadioptric MTO 1000A. Viewing with a long telephoto for the first time is a most exciting experience, and opens up a new wonderworld of photographic possibilities. It often marks the day that a photographer begins to turn out artistic or significant pictures.

The standard lenses supplied with single-lens reflex cameras usually have a closest focusing distance of about 18″.

Fig. 23. The Zenith-E with a specially mounted 300mm f/4.5 Tair-3 lens is designated Photosniper. It can be focused swiftly and held comfortably. Ideal for faces and candids.

By using extension tubes between lens and camera we can enter the world of macro-photography. The three tubes separately give varying degrees of magnification. All together, they enable us to reproduce our subject same size, the ratio being approximately 1:1. This is indeed a wonderful world to explore, where objects small enough to be taken for granted suddenly become imbued with marvellous characteristics. Backlight on a sugar cube becomes the face of a glacier at sunset. A beetle becomes a prehistoric monster. The bee bringing pollen becomes a visual poem in a brown-and-yellow striped jersey!

It is a fascinating world for the collector, too. He can keep photographic records of postage stamps, and other small objects. The botanist can make glorious pictures of sticky buds opening, flowers unfolding, and have the pictures or slides ready for demonstration all the year round.

A bellows unit has the advantage that the degree of image magnification is infinitely variable over a range from 1:2 to 2.5:1 when using the standard lens, but those extension tubes are handy and easy to use.

An idea that won instant acclaim when introduced is the Photosniper, basically an SLR in combination with a 300mm lens in quick-focus mount on a steadying gunstock. Unlike an ordinary SLR the model on the Photosniper has

Fig. 24. Wide-angle lens for Zenith is the 37mm f/2.8 MIR-1. It gives fine rendering of detail at full aperture, with high contrast.

Fig. 25. Wide-angle lens in action. This press picture of a skating star was taken from a low angle to emphasise the skate. Extreme depth of field allows the photographer to fill the foreground.

an additional release button set into the bottom plate. This couples the camera with the shutter release trigger of the gunstock. This camera also has a more extended viewfinder eyepiece, with eyecup, making for more comfortable viewing and focusing with the outfit in the aiming position. Other Pentax-fitting lenses may be used interchangeably with the Photosniper's standard 300mm lens. The focusing screen is bright and evenly illuminated so that the Photosniper outfit can be focused rapidly even indoors. I well remember trying it out at a trade fair when the outfit was first introduced to British photographers. There was no problem in focusing upon people walking inside Olympia, and by resting the hand-held pistol grip on a balustrade my Tri-X negatives were pin-sharp at 1/60th second.

The specially mounted 300mm lens has a spring-loaded pre-set diaphragm which closes automatically to the stopped-down position when you squeeze the trigger release.

The Photosniper is supplied as an impressively complete outfit in a fitted metal case of high quality. The inner side of the lid carries a 58mm f/2 lens under a hermetic cap, 5 filters, two spare film cassettes (a third is supplied in the camera), 2 engineer's screwdrivers, plus a front and back cap.

The camera, with 300mm lens in place, is fastened to a bracket by a clamping screw, while spring clips secure the shoulder butt at the bottom of the case. The case has strong locking catches to prevent accidental opening, a carrying handle and a strong, adjustable shoulder strap. The outfit is supplied with a nicely designed rubber lenshood, very useful in tele-photography, but also protecting the lens in action and rain.

The naturalist will use the Photosniper to scan hedgerows and river bank, revealing their unsuspecting denizens as they go about their business. From his hidden position, he will be able to capture each picture as that of the otter in Fig. 31, where the fierce little fellow is just finishing a fish lunch.

The sports photographer will have his task made easy by the Photosniper's quick focusing, allowing him to concentrate more fully on the action. Rugger players will seem to tackle the lens itself, while the angry words between player and the referee will appear sharper still.

Wide-angle lenses

Characteristic of the wide-angle lens is that it allows you to fill the foreground with an important object, relating it to a wide sweep of background. Suppose, for example, you see an antique horse trough in a village street, on the other side of which stand shops with picturesque thatched roofs. If you wanted to include both the trough and the shops with your standard lens you'd have to walk backwards a fair distance (in order to include all the shops), by which time the trough would have dwindled to insignificance in the middle distance.

By using the wide-angle lens, you can get in close, filling the foreground with the trough. Because of its wide angle of acceptance, the lens will show all the shops with their thatches in the background.

Indoors, too, the wide angle can be invaluable. At parties it allows you to photograph whole groups in quite small rooms, and also lets you show, in a single picture, best part of the rooms themselves.

The amateur who likes to grab life as it is, uses the wide-angle lens just as much as the standard one. The wide angle allows him to get right into the action, at pop festivals, debates, indoor sports and so on, shooting around him at players, involved speakers or contestants. His pictures then have a sense of immediacy and involvement.

Medium telephotos

One of the most valuable lenses in the SLR user's armoury, a lens of 85mm—105mm, fulfils several functions. Its view of things is twice as intimate as that of the standard lens. If it has a large maximum aperture it can be used for available light photography indoors, even in dim conditions. It is thus ideal for the photographer who wants to work unobtrusively, composing natural pictures of whatever is happening around him.

This focal length is exactly right for portraits, as it gives a full head and shoulders with pleasing perspective from

Fig. 26. Jupiter-9, an 85mm f/2, is the most useful telephoto lens for portraiture, sport, and general subjects.

Fig. 27. Isolated against the sky this girl and her dog were given low-angle perspective with the 85mm f/2 Jupiter-9. Excellent colour correction gives extremely clear, well saturated transparencies. Kodachrome film.

Fig. 28. The Jupiter-11 135mm f/4 telephoto is a special optical design. At this focal length it is noted for crisp definition and contrast at all apertures.

Fig. 29. Telemar-22 200mm f/5.6 true telephoto of outstanding performance. It gives high resolution edge-to-edge at full aperture, is very light, and thus extremely popular with outdoor types.

about $4\frac{1}{2}'$. Advanced amateurs and professional portraitists use the lens in conjunction with two or three 500w. photo lamps. With Type B High Speed Ektachrome film, colour portrait slides can be made at 1/60th second, allowing the photographer freedom of movement with a hand-held camera.

One advantage of owning telephoto lenses is that they teach you to be selective. A common fault of most novices is that their pictures contain too much of the surroundings to diminish the effect of the subject proper. A telephoto, by taking in less of the field of view, helps overcome this fault.

135mm telephotos

Of longer focal length still, the 135mm lens is a favourite of sports and press photographers, and pictorialists who wish to concentrate on highly selective areas of the scene before them. This lens will, for example, isolate and fill the frame with that beautiful chestnut tree that cannot be reached across a river, or the tumbledown railway building beyond the lines.

It is used generally for candid photography, and will enable you to take pictures of children at play, people strolling, street buskers, zoo animals, without the necessity for getting too close.

Although interchangeable with the 85mm—105mm as a portrait lens, the 135mm gives a more interesting, because less rounded, full-face portrait. However, you are hardly likely to need both lenses, and the choice should be according to the type of work that attracts you most. Portraiture and available light work: 85mm—105mm. General work, mainly candid and sports: 135mm.

200mm telephotos

A 200mm lens can double for the 135mm, and many prefer it for open air candids. It lets you get in close from a really good distance away, so there is little chance of disturbing human or animal subjects when pointing the lens at them. Preferred by many sports and county show photographers because it allows you to photograph the action taking place in the middle of the stadium or ring.

Fig. 30. With the Tair-3, a 300mm f/4.5 lens, we move into the big league. Very light for such a long lens (about 3 lbs.) it works splendidly alone, or for ultra-fast hand-held sport and candids when incorporated in the Photosniper mount. See Fig. 23.

Fig. 31. The darting movements of this otter as it caught and ate a fish were brought up close and focused swiftly with the Photosniper outfit.

Fig. 32. Easily hand-held, the MTO 500A mirror lens gives magnification equivalent to a cumbersome 500mm lens of normal construction. Aperture f/8.

Fig. 33. The MTO 1000A allows you to fill the 35mm frame with Nelson's face on top of his column, or a goalkeeper from the stands. Aperture f/10.

Fig. 34. MTO 1000A folds up light rays so that this relatively short-mount lens gives same magnification as a conventional but cumbersome 1000mm lens. A true Olympic Stadium performer.

This lens is really the interim optic between those meant for general photography and the 'long toms' with more specialised uses.

300mm—400mm telephotos

Such lenses are just the job for motor racing, stadium sports such as football, and aircraft spotting near your local airfield. With the best ones, definition is crisp at full aperture and contrast good. Lightness of weight is an important consideration, as you will find yourself wilting if you hold a heavy one to your eye for more than half a minute.

Foreshortening, or the flattening of planes, becomes quite pronounced at these focal lengths. From a high viewpoint, for example, parallel streets and traffic streams telescope together into intriguing patterns, aircraft or ships some distance apart come together to form unusual pictures. No one lens can ever be ideal for every subject, and though the 200mm is more generally useful for candids, the longer lens is useful here too. In a situation where the 200mm lens might give you a knee-length picture of a fascinating character, the 300mm or 400mm would fill your frame with just the half-length you were after. There isn't always time

Fig. 35. Filters will improve tonal quality of black and white film, but should be used only when appropriate. Yellow darkens skies, orange even more so, green lightens foliage and is good for suntanned skin.

Fig. 36. The set of four extension tubes for Zenith, or three for Fed and Zorki, enable you to take close-ups of stamps, bees on flowers, and similar subjects up to same-size.

48

Fig. 37. Striking match was taken by daylight with some bounce flash fill-in (see Flash), using a hand-held camera with extension tube behind the standard lens. Close-up facility extends the frontiers of interest and enjoyment.

to walk in closer, and in any case, doing so might alert a self-conscious subject and spoil the photographer's chances.

One point I have always remarked about the service the Russian photographic industry offers its customers, is that accessories are often supplied with the main item at no extra charge, instead of adding to the cost of one's purchase. The longer lenses, for example, are supplied complete with a set of fine optically flat filters inside the hide case. Bought separately, these 77mm screw-in filters would add many pounds to the price.

Mirror lenses

Mirror telephoto lenses work on the catadioptric principle, but before we swallow our tonsils, let me explain. A 500mm or 1000mm telephoto lens of normal construction is a mighty affair that needs a camel to carry it around. It also needs a special heavy tripod designed, in the case of the 1000mm lens, to provide support at more than one point.

In a mirror lens, the rays of light are 'folded' inside the

Fig. 38. Zenith with extension tubes makes close-ups like this easy. With lens extended by tube(s) an exposure increase factor must be applied. See table in Useful Charts.

Fig. 39. Extension tubes allowed Zenith standard lens to be focused this close. Backlighting ensured that spider and web would stand out from background.

Fig. 40. The thinnest extension tube will let you get as close as this. A single flash was used to get depth of field and optimum sharpness. Fall-off in flash power gives contrasting dark background.

Fig. 41. Bellows enable you to magnify the subject considerably more than with extension tubes. These Russian bellows are built to precision standards with twin rails for rigidity. Rear and front standards can be moved independently.

Fig. 42. Leningrad-4 exposure meter. Light but sensitive, it has an accessory incident light attachment carried in the leather case.

Fig. 43. The Etude slide projector throws a really bright picture on the screen. The projection lens, reflector and 100w. lamp combine to give even illumination with edge-to-edge sharpness.

mount by means of an ultra-precision mirror assembly, but cuts down the enormous weight of metal. Thus, the MTO 500A, for example, is only about 175mm long, and weighs only 1250 gms.; while the MTO 1000A is 278mm long, and weighs but 3200 gms.

Although the bigger lens is more manageable on a big tripod or other firm support, the smaller one is well known for its balance—the ease with which it can be hand-held. One could describe the 500mm mirror lens as the lens that gives you a ringside seat from the grandstand, and the 1000mm as the great revealer—the lens which shows you in intimate detail the faraway cricketer on his lonely crease putting the tip of his tongue in the corner of his mouth when facing a fast bowler.

Extension tubes and bellows

Close-up photographs of two or three flowers can be made with the unaided standard lens at the closest focusing

Fig. 44. The single-lens reflex is unsurpassed for the fine focusing required when photographing subjects like this. With short depth of field, especially at wide lens apertures, this fact is appreciated by every naturalist-photographer.

Fig. 45. In order to frame the eggs neatly in the centre of the opening in the twigs above them, a parallax-free camera is required. The single-lens reflex is the obvious answer, as the photographer sees from exactly the same angle as the lens.

Fig. 46. For stage shots you need a wide aperture and medium focal length. The 85mm f/2 Jupiter-9 is the perfect lens for the job.

Fig. 47. The single-lens reflex in close-up photography. A single bloom is often far more effective than a whole bunch. Taken on Kodak Ektachrome film.

Fig. 48. Looking for the unusual can often produce rewarding results, as with this portrait seen in the wing mirror of a car. Only with a camera like the Zenith can you be sure of getting the face positioned exactly right in the mirror.

distance of 18″ or so. To get closer we may use either a supplementary close-up lens screwed to the front of the camera lens, or we may insert an extension ring between lens and camera. The former has the advantage that no increase of exposure is called for, whereas an 'exposure increase factor' must be applied when using extension rings. On the other hand, and to me this has always been the deciding factor, the extension ring does not interfere with the optical performance of the camera lens. The supplementary lens does, especially by reducing fine resolving power at the edge of the field.

A set of three or four extension tubes may be used singly

Fig. 49. Bonfire and fireworks night pictures can be quite striking. Using high speed Ektachrome film you will be able to shoot views similar to this at 1/15th or 1/30th second at f/2.8, depending on the brightness.

or in combination to provide closely stepped magnifications from about 0.35X to 1.0X, filling the frame with subject sizes from about 2.7″ × 4″ to approximately 1″ × 1½″ (same size). The exposure given by the meter must be increased proportionally with the degree of lens extension, i.e. from about 1.8X to 4.0X. Full figures for exposure increase factors are given in Useful Charts.

The best bellows extension unit for the single-lens reflex consists of a twin-bar of rigid metal, with large focusing knob giving fine focus without backlash by rack-and-pinion drive. It should be possible to lock the bellows at either end, allowing camera or lens to be moved independently of each other. There should be a locking ring at the camera end to allow a quick changeover from horizontal to vertical format. Using the standard lens magnification should be continuous between about 1.2X and 2.5X, filling the frame with subject sizes from 0.8″ × 1.2″ to 0.4″ × 0.6″. The exposure meter indication must be increased proportionally with the degree of extension i.e. from 4.8X to 12X. Full figures for exposure increase factors are given in Useful Charts.

People are often puzzled about obtaining an exposure reading for a very small object against a contrasting background, say, a white pearl on black velvet. Naturally, the meter's angle of acceptance is far wider than the pearl, and the black velvet would cause the meter to give a false reading, leading to gross over-exposure of the pearl.

There are two answers, equally efficient. One is to use the incident light method, pointing the meter with incident light attachment from subject position towards the camera. This is fine by daylight, or when using lamps no closer than about three feet. At closer distances you may have to allow for a slight tendency towards under-exposure as the meter, raised towards the camera, will be closer to the lights than is the subject.

An accurate reflected light reading is made by placing a sheet of matt mid-grey art paper, or brown wrapping paper, over the subject while taking a reading.

Well, that is the average SLR system, not priding itself on having every gimmick known to man, but containing every essential for general and specialist photography from macro- to telephotography, from clutch of eggs to stadium, from family party to medical research.

Having made your colour slides you will want to view them, and the delightful little Etude projector is ideal for the purpose, hardly bigger than a table viewer and can, in fact, be carried in a briefcase or kept on a table ready to project a small picture, say 12″ wide, on any convenient white viewing surface. At the same time, it will give a bright 3′ wide screen image in a darkened room at a screen-projector distance of 7′ 6″.

The Etude is just 6″ × 2″ × 4″ closed, and weighs only 28 ozs. It has an 80mm f/2.8 projection lens, and the light is provided by a 100-watt 240-volt projection lamp in fixed position before a parabolic reflector. There is a triple condenser system with heat absorbing glass between the front two lenses, the whole unit being contained within a series of baffles. Ventilation is such that no fan-cooling is required, which contributes to the remarkably low price. Slides are changed manually in a simple push-pull carrier.

Rangefinder

The rangefinder camera provides the fastest and most positive method of bringing a lens into focus. There's much truth in the old hand's saying that the single-lens reflex is satisfactory for focusing, superb for viewing, while the rangefinder camera is superb for focusing, satisfactory for viewing. Human beings being human, some prefer one, some the other, and some both. Pressmen certainly prefer both. They recognise the view-power of the SLR, and the great advantage of the rangefinder—it lets you snap into focus in dim light, especially when using a wideangle at full aperture.

In these pages we examine the advantages of the rangefinder camera for the candid quick shot; as a press camera; its use with wide-angle and telephoto lenses, and their suitability for different kinds of photography.

Fig. 50. The Fed-3 with f/2.8 lens is a modestly-priced rangefinder camera, ideal for the beginner, but perfectly capable of producing the highest quality results. The Industar 4-element lens is renowned for sharpness and good contrast even at full aperture.

Fig. 51. Similar to the Fed-3 is the Fed-4 which has a built-in exposure meter. In other respects, the two cameras are identical. They have Leica-type screw thread lenses, so other accessories with this thread may be used.

Rangefinder

Any professional will tell you that the rangefinder camera can be focused faster and more accurately than any other type of camera. The point is, when using a ground-glass screen, however bright, one rocks the focus back and forth, relying on one's own sharpness of vision to decide at what point optimum sharpness has been reached. With the rangefinder you simply superimpose two images and focus is spot on. Both methods work, but the rangefinder way is the high speed way. Before discussing the extent and scope of the rangefinder system, let us take a look at the camera itself.

There are many fixed-lens cameras of high quality which focus by rangefinder and they serve the out-and-about needs of the hobbyist. On the other hand, there are very few 'system' models. Best known are the superb and classical Leica which started the whole business of 35mm photography, and the Russian Fed and Zorki models.

The system rangefinder camera with interchangeable lenses is often used by pressmen, who need to get into action fast. Some press photographers start off the morning or afternoon by applying to aperture ring and shutter speed knob the indication given by their meter and continue to take pictures at the same setting. A fresh meter reading is taken as a check on the light level perhaps once an hour, or if an obvious change occurs, such as a bank of cloud obscuring the sun. This is a method in which the budding photo-journalist can have confidence when working in black and white, as this has more exposure tolerance than colour film. With colour, though, always use the meter whenever time allows.

A shutter speed of 1/1000th second is useful in certain kinds of sports photography. It is worth bearing in mind, though, that the photography of racing cars and similar subjects is usually done with a panning motion of the camera, in which the subject is held central in the moving viewfinder. Even a shutter speed of 1/250th second is sufficient to render the subject sharply, while imparting a moderate lateral blur to the background, which gives an excellent impression of speed.

For this reason, professional photographers of car and motorcycle racing seldom use a faster speed than 1/500th second, the top speed on some cameras. In a picture of a diver, say, where it is desirable to show the background of spectators sharply, as well as the diver, or during a long jump where a similar effect is required, the bonus speed of 1/1000th second can be very useful.

The top speed of 1/500th second on some cameras, however, is adequate for the vast majority of action pictures.

The standard lens on most rangefinder cameras is usually a 50mm f/2, corrected to give crispness and good resolution at the larger apertures. It is ideal for working indoors without flash, at dances and parties, and under any conditions where the use of flash would be distracting. Used at more modest apertures, it will serve for pictorial photography as well as those lenses of more modest maximum aperture.

Fig. 52. The Zorki-4 has a highly corrected 6-element f/2 Jupiter lens with excellent performance at full aperture, and a shutter speed range to 1/1000th second. Rangefinder cameras like Fed and Zorki focus faster than cameras with other focusing systems.

The accessory lenses for rangefinder cameras are in focal lengths from 21mm (Leica M) to 135mm and between them they cover every need of the rangefinder photographer. The longest focal length of 135mm is ideal for most medium to long distance work, but those whose interests lie in extreme telephotography will obviously choose the SLR system, with longer focal lengths of 200mm, 300mm, 500mm and 1000mm.

21mm—28mm lenses

The 21mm is a very specialised lens, and the 28mm focal length with a 75° field of view is normally the widest angle lens with rangefinder fitting for general use. It is valuable to the architectural photographer, partly because it will take in a broad field from a restricted distance, and partly because the tops of tall buildings may be included without having to tilt the camera upwards, with the result that the vertical lines will converge.

The 28mm is frequently chosen by photo-journalists or

Fig. 53. When using rangefinder cameras with lenses of non-standard focal length, viewing of the subject may be done through this Universal Viewfinder, which shows correct framing for five different focal lengths up to 135mm.

Fig. 54. The Orion-15 is a 28mm f/6 wide-angle lens for Fed and Zorki. Not only does it allow you to get a great deal in when space is limited, but it also produces striking creative effects.

Fig. 55. The Jupiter-12, 35mm f/2.8 is the most useful wide-angle lens for general work. Seen here in mount for Fed and Zorki. This focal length is often used as 'standard' by pressmen and pictorialists.

Fig. 56. The Jupiter-9 is the lens for the action photographer, especially where the light is dim. Of 85mm focal length and with a maximum aperture of f/2, it is an equal favourite with the 135mm f/4 Jupiter-11 for landscape work, though the shorter lens scores for portraiture.

amateurs who like to photograph 'life as it is lived'. Its use enables the photographer to move in very close to his subjects, perhaps with the camera held unobtrusively at hip or chest level, and photograph people up tight. There is a feeling of participation and engagement about pictures taken in this way with the 28mm which is unique to this short focal length.

35mm lenses

The most popular wide-angle lens for rangefinder photography, the 35mm ends up being used as standard equipment by many photographers who come to recognise its worth. It has an angle of acceptance of 63° and with a maximum aperture of f/2.8, f/2 or f/1.4, it can enter successfully the many 'speed' fields of photography. At the same time, it is a favourite of landscape photographers because its great depth of field and wide angle allow the inclusion of a foreground object and those in the distance to be shown in relation to each other. The better quality 35mm lenses work well at full aperture and give edge-to-edge coverage when stopped down to f/4 or thereabouts.

Performance is nearly distortion-free. The medium contrast and good definition become really impressive at f/8.

Fig. 57. The Jupiter-11 is a Sonnar-type lens with maximum aperture f/4. Its 135mm focal length produces a distortion-free, crisp result of good contrast. Favoured for sports and candids, and good for full-head portraits.

85mm—90mm lenses

Probably the most useful and popular lenses in the range, with maximum apertures of f/2. That means that performers on stage, animals at the zoo, even in heavily shaded corners, can be photographed with ease.

At the same time, these are good general purpose lenses and cannot be bettered for portraiture.

Perhaps the most important aspect of the 85mm or 90mm f/2, and one which is not mentioned in the specifications, is that it balances well in the hand when attached to the front of the camera. It seems to form an integral unit with the photographer, making it easy to hold

Fig. 58. The out-and-about photographer should keep an eye open—and his camera ready—for natural subjects like this sleeping fireman at a fairground. Take an exposure reading and set the camera from time to time, so that you need only focus and shoot.

Fig. 59. Subjects like this won't wait for you to get ready. They're gone in a moment, so keep the lens and shutter speed set, and the camera with wide-angle lens focused at, say, 6′. You can then 'grab' anything that happens up to 10′ away with reasonable sharpness.

Fig. 60. Another example of the kind of picture that attracts the man who likes photo-journalism. Whether you use Rangefinder Fed or Zorki, or SLR Zenith, have the camera set for action when in a place with high picture potential.

Fig. 61. The wide-angle lens ensures that you'll get the subject all in (no pun intended) with sufficient depth of field.

Fig. 62. Children and animals are the most popular subjects in photography, and this shot on Ektachrome film combines the two. Note how the touch of action raises this above a mere snapshot.

Fig. 63. Use a fast black and white film for dull weather photo-journalism. This Irish wolfhound is fairly steady, but a moment later a fast shutter speed was needed as he raced away.

still during relatively long exposures. Pressmen who are used to working at exposures of 1/15th and even 1/8th second when this is unavoidable indoors, much appreciate this aspect of the lens. 90mm lenses of more modest maximum aperture are available, and these are popular with those for whom the ultimate in speed is not essential.

135mm lenses

The longest lens in the rangefinder user's armoury is the 135mm telephoto. Where the 85mm—90mm focal length excels for head and shoulder portraiture, the 135mm will fill

Fig. 64. High speed Ektachrome film enables you to take pictures under ring lighting at 1/60th second at f/2. Pressmen use this 125 ASA artificial-light type film at 500 ASA and have it specially processed, so exposures can be even faster.

the frame with just a face. For that exquisite, revealing portrait of a very old lady, the 135mm is the lens *par excellence*.

It is also an excellent focal length for the photographer who takes his sport and candid work seriously. Remember, that with a rangefinder camera, the maximum aperture of the lens has no effect on the ease of focusing. Whereas an 85mm f/2 will focus more easily on a single-lens reflex than, say, an f/2.8, the same does not apply when focusing by rangefinder. The image in the optical viewfinder remains

Fig. 65. The standard lens of 50mm—58mm focal length will cope with 90% of the situations you meet. With a good action colour shot such as this one of mechanics 'winding up' a Fairey Swordfish, accurate exposure is essential.

Fig. 66. This unpleasant surprise for the motorists who ignored the warning 'Don't park— tidal creek', was taken in the shade of the trees, without sun. Use of a UV filter protects colour film from a blue cast in such conditions.

just as bright whatever the maximum aperture. This is why the 135mm f/4 with its limited depth of field, and the 28mm with enormous depth of field, snap into focus with equal ease.

Universal viewfinder

This clips into the accessory shoe and gives the correct field framing for each of the lenses in the range. Five focal lengths from 28mm to 135mm are covered. The turret-head type viewfinder operates on the telescope principle. One rotates the head, bringing a new viewfinder lens into place for each desired focal length. The frame size remains the same, but the image is magnified accordingly. Needless to say, the image is far easier to relate to the effect the camera lens will have on the film. Provision is made for parallax compensation at closer distances.

Extension Tubes

Precision machined tubes are available to fit rangefinder cameras with old Leica-type screw fitting. These enable reproduction ratios up to 1:1. Distances from subject plane to focal plane must be measured accurately. A table giving reproduction ratios and exposure increase factors will be found in Useful Charts.

Special Cameras

There are some things the normal 35mm camera cannot do. It cannot, for example, take a single-exposure panoramic view without distortion; it cannot produce the same quality at high degrees of enlargement as a bigger camera, when both are using fast film; it cannot produce the large colour transparencies that some publishers and magazine editors prefer. For these and other reasons, a certain number of specialist cameras have been designed to fulfil these functions.

This short chapter is mainly concerned with the 6 × 6cm single-lens reflex and the panoramic camera.

Fig. 67. The camera for the professional or advanced amateur who wants the ultimate in picture quality at high degrees of enlargement. The Zenith-80 has inter-changeable magazines, and apart from its standard 80mm f/2.8 lens, has an inter-changeable 65mm wide-angle and a 300mm telephoto lens.

Fig. 68. To obtain the utmost in fine detail, especially when your colour transparency is for reproduction in the press, the 6 × 6cm format of the Zenith-80 cannot be bettered. The Zenith-80's viewing screen makes low angle shooting more comfort-able. Shot on Ektachrome.

Fig. 69. The Mir-3 is the Zenith-80's wide-angle lens. A 65mm f/3.5 highly corrected 6-element lens, it has high definition and good contrast. It is supplied complete with two 88mm filters in hide case.

Fig. 70. The Tair-33 is the Zenith-80's telephoto lens. Of 300mm focal length, it balances well for hand-held photography. With maximum aperture f/4.5 it is a favourite lens at sporting events.

Special Cameras
The Zenith-80

With the same shape and appearance as the world's top status symbol camera of this type, the Zenith-80 is a 6 × 6cm single-lens reflex with 80mm f/2.8 Industar-29 lens, specially computed for this camera. It is a construction of 4 elements arranged in 3 groups, and is noted for the pleasing roundness it imparts to portraits.

When the release button is pressed, the following sequence of events takes place: (1) the lens diaphragm stops down to the pre-set stop; (2) the mirror flies up out of the light-path; (3) the stainless steel focal plane shutter makes its traverse.

A turn of the large milled wind-on knob does three things: (1) lowers the mirror into the viewing position again; (2) winds on the film one frame; (3) cocks the shutter. A very functional point is the shutter speed change, incorporated in the same wind-on knob. The diaphragm is re-opened by cocking a spring lever on the lens mount.

The Zenith-80 outfit includes two roll film magazines for 12 exposures. One can change from black and white to colour at will and, of course, any number of magazines may be carried. The camera incorporates some quite sophisticated devices: separate film counter on the magazine; magazine cannot be removed until sheath is inserted; shutter cannot be fired until sheath is withdrawn; indicator windows for 'shutter set' and 'film wound'; novel sunk lenshood secures filters; auto numbering by film counter on magazine; two-action release erects hood first, then magnifier.

Accessory lenses for the Zenith-80 are perhaps the two most useful extra focal lengths for this format. There is a

Fig. 71. The Lubitel-2 twin-lens reflex is an excellent camera for the beginner, who can see in the large, bright screen just what he is trying for. Its big screen is also a useful way of learning to compose a picture well.

Fig. 72. This girl-and-doll portrait was taken with a twin-lens camera like the Lubitel-2. Note the strength imparted by the diagonal composition. Taken indoors near a window.

65mm f/3.5 Mir-3 for wide-angle work, and a 300mm f/4.5 Tair-33. Both are very highly corrected and, like the standard lens, each is supplied complete with filters in the lens case.

Lubitel-2

An extremely versatile 6 × 6cm twin-lens focusing reflex taking twelve pictures on 120 roll film. Although this camera

Fig. 73. The Cosmic-35 is a basic 35mm camera with scale focusing by rotating the f/4 lens. Very low in price, but very high in performance, as you can see in the picture taken with it in Fig. 74.

Fig. 74. This model was posed on a roll of white paper in an ordinary drawing room, and lit by a single flash reflected from the ceiling. Taken on the low-price, high-performance Cosmic-35 camera.

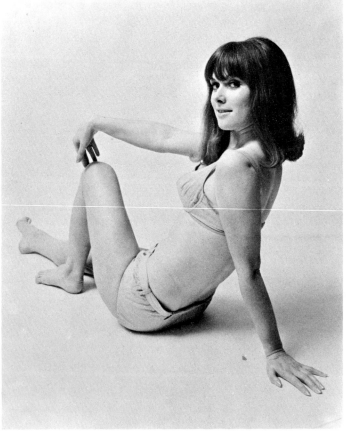

Fig. 75. A specialist camera, the Horizont has a revolving lens/shutter that 'sweeps' the film held in a curved plane, to produce a completely distortion-free picture 24mm × 58mm.

Fig. 76. An example of the kind of picture you can take with the Horizont camera. The viewfinder incorporates a spirit level, enabling you to hold the camera level for distortion-free results. If you wish, you can purposely tilt the camera to make startling distortions.

is priced at the lower end of the scale, it incorporates most features required by the keen beginner and yet has a performance that will satisfy the critical user.

The lens is a 75mm coated f/4.5, which focuses down to 4′. The leaf shutter is behind the lens, has five speeds from 1/15th to 1/250th second, and is synchronised for flash.

The Lubitel-2 is a camera without frills. You wind on the film by means of an ordinary knob and there is a window to show you the frame numbering on the film backing paper. There is a clever helical screw mount to the taking lens. As this is rotated it turns the upper, viewing lens to similar focus. Viewing is by means of an always-in-focus convex lens giving a brilliant image. A circular ground-glass spot at the centre is used for focusing. There is a folding magnifier and a flip-up direct vision viewfinder incorporated in the folding hood. The camera *contains* a filter compartment, has a delayed action device built into the shutter, and is supplied with ever-ready case.

Cosmic-35

This camera has a quite remarkable specification at its very low price, and is capable of producing very high quality work. It was used by the author to produce the glamour shot seen in Fig. 74, with bounce-flash used to light the model against a white paper roll background. Using 35mm film, the Cosmic-35 has a 40mm f/4 coated lens of three elements set in a helical focusing mount. Focusing is down to 3'. There is a direct vision optical viewfinder. The shutter is leaf-type, set behind the lens, and shutter speeds are B, 1/15th, 1/30th, 1/60th, 1/125th and 1/250th second. Delayed action device gives you about 9 seconds to get into your own picture—without the camera of course.

Horizont

A special panoramic camera fitted with a rotating built-in lens that 'sweeps' the curved film plane, providing a distortion-free picture 24mm × 58mm. It will take 10 pictures on 20-exposure film, 20 on 36-exposure film. Angular view of the special f/2.8 28mm lens is a full 120° in the horizontal plane, 45° in the vertical plane. Exact framing is not possible with such a wide-angle camera, due to variables in eye position and acceptance angles, but excellent guided viewing is through a special optical viewfinder incorporating an all-important spirit level.

Nominal shutter speeds are 1/30th, 1/60th and 1/125th second, though setting these merely adjusts the shutter blind slit. Speed of traverse of the lens remains the same. The Horizont has obvious applications in architectural and planning work, but the amateur and professional seeking new effects will find the Horizont able to provide everything from unusual panoramas to intentional distortions of remarkable impact.

Enlarging

Enlarging from a negative can be a creative act, and we should look upon enlarging as something more than merely a way of making pictures bigger. Although certain aspects of what we saw in a scene, the play of wintry sun on swirling russet leaves, the social statement of old boots left on a park bench, incited us to take the picture in the first place, the memory fades and the details that excited us are awfully small on a negative. During the enlarging process the excitement of the subject is revealed to us again on the baseboard and it is at this stage that we finalise the picture which is our communication of the event or object to our viewers. Our printing method, choice of paper, sticking to or departing from the composition of the negative, will all influence the mood and effect of the visual statement. Where the painter goes from vision to canvas, we go from vision to enlarging paper via a negative. It affords us a great deal of control and is the photographic equivalent of the painter's freehand drawing.

This chapter does two things: it shows you how to develop the aesthetic approach to enlarging, so that your photographs will be real pictures; it also teaches you how to master the technical side of enlarging, so that you can print the way you want, without fuss.

Enlarging

A complete course of enlarging know-how, divided into three parts for your convenience.

PART 1: AESTHETICS

'A good big un' will always beat a good 'little un' was never more true than in the field of photographic enlarging. Pressmen have long known the psychological effect on editors of a set of 12″ × 15″ prints. Size alone, though, is not the secret of success. For a mature appreciation, memorise the following considerations, under the general heading *Aesthetics of Enlarging*:

(1) Correct enlarged size for your purpose.
(2) Adjustment of frame to suit subject.
(3) Correction or implementation of negative image.
(4) Chosen contrast and depth.
(5) Paper surface and weight.
(6) Flush or border presentation.

Let's deal with these aesthetic considerations.

1. Correct size

If you want a *literal* effect in the print, with perspective appearing normal, view the print from such a distance that the angle to your eye approximates the acceptance angle of the lens. For example, a 50-55mm lens on 35mm, or an 80mm lens on 6 × 6cm, has an acceptance angle of about 45°. The diagonal of an 8″ × 10″ print is about 12¾″, and will look normal when held about 15½″ from the eye.

Here are conventionally correct viewing distances for various sizes of print from negatives made with a lens of standard focal length:

Print size	6½″	8½″	10″	12″	15″	20″
Viewing distance	9½″	13″	15½″	19″	23″	31″

As the eye cannot focus easily under about 9″, it follows that enlargements under 5″ × 7″ cannot be viewed in 'correct' perspective. But don't stick slavishly to what is supposedly correct or normal. Pictures are what you make

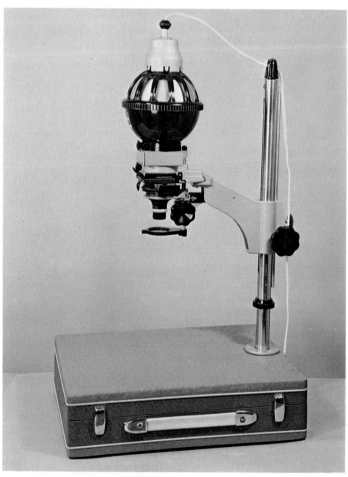

Figs. 77, 78. Zenith UPA-5 enlarger focuses automatically up to 8X magnification, after which focusing is manual. With quality 4-element enlarging lens, well-made single-glass 35mm carrier, the enlarger packs away for storage in the carrying case which forms its baseboard.

Fig. 79. Although composition, should be arranged at the taking stage, enlarging affords the opportunity to adjust composition for effective results. Here, boy and girl walk dynamically in from edge of frame.

them, and their success is the impact they have on the viewer.

2. Adjustment of frame

Many photographers are in the habit of *fitting the enlarged area to the paper shape*, instead of the other way round. If you always use the full paper shape, you will get in the habit of composing accordingly. In fact, you should choose the shape of your print to suit the subject—a fact you should bear in mind while composing in the viewfinder at the taking stage. Long narrow subjects call for long narrow prints. Squares are best suited to static subjects and ones that fall naturally into that shape. But don't start getting wayout simply for the sake of being different, using triangle and keyhole shape frames. Note that classic and even modern painters seldom depart from the rectangular frame, but they suit the actual proportions to their subject.

3. Correcting the image

Provided the eye behind the viewfinder of the modern miniature is experienced, the small screen of the SLR is a sufficient aid to composition. Not perfect, because the depth of field we see can look different on an enlarged print.

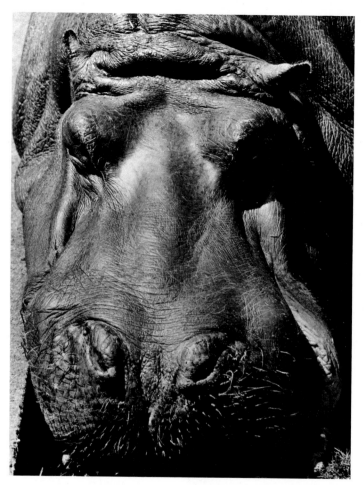

Fig. 80. This picture of a Hippo's head was cropped in very close for maximum impact. Beautiful sunlit texture was captured on 120 Agfa ISS film.

Also, the elongated 2:3 shape of a 35mm negative is not ideal for most compositions. Precisely because we *can't* compose perfectly at the taking stage, we tend to be a bit haphazard, relying on corrections in the darkroom.

Golden rule: compose as accurately as you can at the taking stage, to minimise the amount of correction needed at the enlarging stage.

4. Contrast and depth

Avoid bittiness, any confusing detail that doesn't actually aid the composition. Pictorial rule: simplify and eliminate. A few bold light and dark masses offsetting each other make more impact than lots of objects and tones. With subjects of delicate tone the balancing of masses becomes quite critical. Only a small patch of heavy tone is needed to balance a large light area. No matter whether the darkest tone required in a picture is pale grey or black, *richness* of tone can be achieved only by full paper development. Here is a point where aesthetics are directly controlled by technique.

5. Paper surface and weight

A practical consideration is that a black and white print on paper has a tonal range of only 1:30 or so, whereas the tonal range of the subject might be ten times as much. Best possible separation of delicate gradations is achieved on glossy paper. So is optimum sharpness and detail. Conversely, tinted papers cut tonal range, and broken surfaces lessen definition.

6. Flush or border presentation

Don't print with regular $\frac{1}{4}''$ white borders simply because your enlarging paper mask is made that way. Let the picture speak for itself. If it *needs* a fancy border or mount, it isn't a self-sufficient picture. The work of great painters is presented often in ornate gold frames. True, but don't let us confuse home decoration with true art.

Editors don't care whether a print has a border or not. It certainly won't end up in print with one. For borderless prints you have two choices. A special borderless easel, or pins in the baseboard. Or, print with a border, then trim it off. Singleweight glossy looks and handles well only when glazed. Unglazed glossy should be doubleweight. Of course, a border is necessary if a print is to be mounted flush, as both print and mount will finally be trimmed.

Fig. 81. Good contrast not only
makes a picture stand out, it
can also be used to create a
strong composition. Exposure
here was for boy in small
clearing. When enlarging,
surround was allowed to go
quite black.

PART 2: MECHANICS

To do its job well, an enlarger must conform to the following technical requirements:

(1) It must provide perfectly even illumination to all areas of the print.

(2) The negative must be held flat without buckling.

(3) The lens must be capable of flat field projection, so that every part of the image can be focused at the same time.

(4) If a condenser is used, this must be parallel with negative and baseboard.

Fig. 82. Use of high contrast enlarging paper removes most half tones. Resulting stark, black and white effect reveals strong pattern of subject without interference or 'dilution' caused by half tones.

(5) The enlarger head must be free from vibration while the enlargement is being made.

1. Illumination

In most enlargers there is a straight-through system, with lamp, condensers, lens, sharing a common axis. An opalized lamp can be raised or lowered on an adjustable standard to give optimum evenness of illumination. Even on the best enlargers of this type illumination is seldom perfectly even until the lens has been stopped down ready for the exposure.

2. Negative flatness

The ideal negative carrier holds the negative flat and prevents it buckling out of focus as it warms up. It can do this in two ways. One, by using glass plates in the carrier

itself. Two, by having the lower plano condenser face hold the negative flat against a rectangular opening in the carrier. The single glass negative carrier is easier to keep clean than sandwich-type carriers, and completely eliminates negative curvature.

3. Enlarger lens

A poor enlarger lens cannot reproduce a flat field. A good one most certainly can, will give good contrast and be quite free from that bugbear of cheap enlarging lenses— astigmatism. At two stops down, in fact at an aperture that gives one sufficient time to control enlarging exposure, some modestly priced enlarging lenses are in no way inferior to the most costly professional ones.

4. Parallel baseboard

Anyone who has ever corrected converging verticals by tilting the paper mask in a direction opposed to that of the convergence, will know that perfect parallelism of the lens, carrier, condenser and lamp is not needed. Nevertheless, for big degrees of enlargement, especially with fine detail at the edges of the print, it is to be desired.

5. Vibration-free enlarging

To avoid providing really massive girder supports, enlarger manufacturers supply columns which are less than rigid. The effect of enlarger vibration during exposure is

Fig. 83. Again, high contrast enlarging paper has been used to eliminate half tones and concentrate the eye on the pattern of these leaves.

Fig. 84. Softness in this instance was obtained by using Eylure make-up and a piece of nylon between lens and paper for half the exposure.

particularly noticeable with big enlargements, when the enlarger head is raised near the top of the column. To cure any possibility of vibration, push the enlarger back towards the wall as far as it will go, and secure the column top against a small block of wood. Even a rubber sponge wedged between wall and column top will damp vibration effectively.

PART 3: TECHNIQUE

Reduced to a formula, enlarging technique can be defined this way:

CHOOSE THE RIGHT PAPER. GIVE JUST ENOUGH EXPOSURE. DEVELOP FULLY.

You can go into your darkroom now, and however poor your printing quality was in the past, you will make richly toned prints after carrying out the following little lesson I have devised for beginners and improvers alike. Simply equip yourself with three packets of 8″ × 10″ bromide paper, glossy surface, grades 1, 2 and 3 (soft, normal, hard) of the same make, and a good print developer.

Fig. 85. By using a relatively high camera position, the cornfield has here been used as a background for this shot of a pretty girl. Not only does the corn complement the blue shirt and red shorts, it also eliminates fussy skyline details.

Fig. 86. By coming closer, the corn is used as a frame for the portrait. Both this and the previous picture are from Kodachrome slides.

Choose a negative you consider of normal density and contrast, and make the best possible print on normal grade paper. Use the whole sheet of paper and develop it *fully*, even if it goes as black as the ace of spades. If too dark, make a second print on the same grade, giving less exposure. If too light, give more exposure. In either case, develop *fully*. According to makers' instructions, that is about 2 minutes at room temperature of about 20°C. (68°F.).

Having made the best possible print on normal paper, and fixed it, examine it in white light. Decide whether the particular negative would have been better printed on softer or harder paper. If the print is harsh with dense blacks, empty highlights and very few half tones, repeat the process on soft paper. If the print is full of detail in the half tones but lacking a satisfying black or a clean white, repeat the process on hard paper.

This little lesson will teach you all about getting the best out of any negative, and will stand you in good stead every time you make enlargements.

Fig. 87. The eye is selective. It can look at each of the flowers in a bed individually. The camera cannot do this, and produces a hotch-potch of irritating colours. Fruit salad is all right to eat, but doesn't make good colour shots.

Fig. 88. Compare this simple pattern of yellow flowers with the mixed-up appearance of the variegated flowers in the previous picture. Ektachrome film.

Flash

Light, according to a dictionary definition, is the agent that excites the eye. For the photographer it is only exciting when full of quality. Light, especially the purely photographic form known as flash, is too often used in quantity rather than quality. The softness of pearly light filtering through trees on a Summer morning, or the theatrical effect of strong backlighting, the buttery glow of sunlight on a girl's skin or the eye-socket shadows of a bare light bulb suspended in a bleak room—all these can be simulated by correct use of flash lighting. Flash is an action-stopping light and a lively light. It can also be an unobtrusive or creative light.

How to calculate flash exposures; balance flash with daylight; get the flash off the camera; use bounce flash for natural effects; disadvantages of electronic or bulb flash compared.

Flash

Flash, like everything else in photography, should be used with imagination. With a flashgun on the camera, its light can be strictly utilitarian. Handled in the way I shall describe, it can provide an almost endless range of interesting and creative effects.

Most modern flashguns, whether electronic or bulb, have a calculator. You simply turn an index to the ASA rating of the film in use, and read off the correct aperture at any distance. This obviates the need to work by the Guide Number system. Just as a reminder, a Guide Number (GN) is supplied by the manufacturer of a flashbulb or electronic unit, to indicate its power. Simply divide the distance from flash to subject into this Guide Number and the answer is your correct lens aperture.

Thus, GN 110, distance 10′, would be aperture f/11. If you can't find a Guide Number (as the lawyers say, hereinafter referred to as GN) for an electronic unit, simply set the calculator for the film in use and multiply any pair of aperture and distance marks. So, if I set the calculator of a particular electronic unit for a given ASA rating, I may get, for example:

at 5′—f/16   at 10′—f/8   at 20′—f/4

Multiply any pair and we have a GN 80. GN's are also provided on the side of flashbulb packages, or can be worked out in the same way.

Windows

I want you to imagine that you are in a room, ready to take a portrait of someone sitting on a window seat with their back to the window. Obviously, the daylight scene outside is going to be very many times brighter than the reflected light on the face of your sitter. If you make a general reflected light exposure reading from a few feet away, the bright window scene will inflate the reading, and the face will be much under-exposed. If you go in close and take a reading from the face alone, the face will be correctly exposed and the scene outside many times over-exposed.

Now take a look at Fig. 94, where similar conditions existed, but we have managed to balance exposure for the

Fig. 89. Flash on the camera is convenient for parties and quick groups, but is a strictly utilitarian form of lighting. It also causes 'red-eye' in portraits.

Fig. 90. By holding the flash away from the camera on a short extension lead, better modelling is obtained, and the shadows can be placed wherever you please.

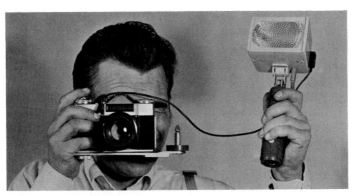

Fig. 91. This is bounce flash, with the flash itself pointing up at the ceiling. The method of obtaining the right exposure is fully described in the section on Bounce Flash.

exterior and the interior. How? Simple. We were using a
film of 125 ASA, and the camera-to-subject distance was 7′.
With a GN 154 divided by 7, we have aperture f/22. Now
we took an exposure reading for the exterior scene and got
these readings:

1/30th at f/22   1/60th at f/16   1/125th at f/11   1/250th,
etc. . . .

Thus, if we set the shutter for 1/30th, the exterior will be
correctly exposed by daylight, the portrait correctly exposed
by flash. With electronic flash, *any* shutter speed would do
on a leaf or front-lens shutter, provided you are plugged in
to the X contact, but with focal plane shutters you are
limited to 1/30th or so. The information is in the instruction
books for particular cameras.

Fig. 92. This picture of a Mother telling a bedtime story to the children was taken with a single flash off to the right of the camera on an extension lead. Because the flash was at some distance, background is fairly well exposed, too. Ektachrome film.

Fig. 93. Film star Barbara Bouchet was photographed indoors by means of bounce flash from a 120-joules electronic flash unit. Note that rear lighting from a window aids the modelling.

To use a larger stop, simply use an extension lead to remove the flash farther from the subject, leaving the camera where it is. Remember, though, the GN depends on the flash-to-subject distance.

Straight flash

Flash on the camera is probably the easiest way to light a subject but it is also the least interesting. Dead flat and uninteresting, and with a nasty habit of joining your sitter to the wall by means of a heavy black shadow. You simply focus the camera, read off the distance on the scale, and set your flash calculator accordingly. This gives you the correct aperture. For groups at parties it works well enough but with colour it causes the phenomenon known as red-eye. Being almost on the same axis as the camera lens, the flash reflects from the eye into the camera, resulting in a red spot.

Pressmen often have no alternative but to use flash on the camera, because of the speed at which they work, but always prefer to work with the camera held in one hand, the flash at the end of a short extension lead held in the other. This

gives far more modelling to the subject, and the result is far more pleasing.

Flash off the camera

In Figs. 89, 90 and 91, we can see three ways of working with flash. Fig. 89 is straightforward flash on camera. Fig. 90 shows the flash being held to one side. If your flash trigger lead is only a few inches long, you can obtain a 3′ extension lead from your dealer. You can also obtain, if you wish, a 12′ or 15′ extension lead. This enables you to put the flash on a stand, a tripod, or a clamp attached to chairback or picture rail. You can then roam around taking photographs at the end of your lead. Whatever the camera-to-subject distance, the flash-to-subject distance remains constant, and there is no need to keep changing the aperture. See Fig. 91.

You may wonder how the chap in Fig. 91 manages to wind on the camera after taking a picture, as he has both hands full. It's really quite easy. As the camera is on a neckstrap, simply press it against your body and wind on

Fig. 94. Balance the exterior daylight with the interior flash light for portraits like this one, taken with the sitter's back to a window.

Fig. 95. This portrait was made with two flashes. One is fairly close to the side and slightly to the rear. The other, near the camera, is being used for filling-in the shadows. This lighting is rather theatrical.

Fig. 96. Use simple flash on the camera, or very close to it, to make mirror portraits like this. The mirror provides a profile with interesting lighting, and you get two portraits for the price of one.

with the hand holding the flash. It works quite well. Of course, you'll need to practise for a few minutes until you can manage a firm one-hand grip on the camera. You'll find that you can also focus the lens with the hand holding the flash.

Bounce flash

The most popular kind of flash with many professionals and advanced amateurs is bounce flash. You see in Fig. 91 the flash held off camera and directed upwards towards the ceiling. From there, the light comes back in diffused form, giving the effect of natural room lighting. Of course, it has the advantage of stopping much more action, and, if the flash is bright enough, having far more depth of field.

The effect can be seen in Fig. 97. You can also make bounce flash pictures by leaving the flash on a stand or clamp, or even resting on the sideboard pointing upwards, while you move around at the end of a long extension lead.

Exposure is no problem. Simply open up the lens two stops bigger than you would need for direct flash at 10′, and the answer is good enough for average rooms. Only if the

Fig. 97. A children's Yoga class conducted by a lady teacher had plenty of daylight, but not enough to stop down the lens for depth of field. With bounce flash from the ceiling, it was possible to use a small aperture.

room is extremely large, or the ceiling browned with smoke, will you need to open the lens about half a stop more. Conversely, in quite small light-walled rooms (such as when photographing the children in the bath) you need open the lens only one stop. Incidentally, the rule about opening the aperture two stops more than for direct flash at 10′ holds good whatever the distance of the flash from the subject. When working very close to the subject with hand-held bounce flash, make sure that the flashgun is held high enough above the shoulder not to spill direct light on to the subject.

By way of guidance, if you are working in an average room with AG1B or PF1B flashbulbs, or one of the many small one-piece electronic units, with a 125 ASA film in the camera, your correct exposure will be in the region of f/4 with the shutter set at 1/30th second. With a powerful press flash of 120-joules output and a film of 400 ASA, you can bounce flash at about f/11.

One advantage of the leaf-shutter type camera is that with bulbs, faster shutter speeds may be used, and GNs for these

Fig. 98. This picture of a beer keller was taken with two direct flashes linked together. One is in front, the other at the side. This form of light is good for large, dark subject areas.

are given on the side of the flashbulb packs. These cameras also allow you to use electronic flash at all shutter speeds. Fig. 99 was made by bounce flash on a very simple camera of this type.

Twin-flash

Years ago, before bounce flash became the most popular light in Fleet Street, twin-flash was used for a great deal of magazine photography. The effect is rather dramatic and theatrical, as you can see in Fig. 95, where one flash has been used from the front to fill-in the shadows cast by the second flash at the side and a bit to the rear. It was also used to make the beer keller picture in Fig. 98.

Twin-flash is a great help when you want something better than a single direct flash, but the ceiling is too high for bounce flash.

First, you need to visit a good dealer and ask to see two different kinds of flash outfit. First, a unit which has an outlet socket to take an accessory extension flash unit. Such extensions usually divide the total flash output with the main flash. Working with the extension off to one side, you use a GN for the front flash alone.

Second, you can use a pair of flash outfits, using a small slave unit to trigger one by the light of the other. These vary in sensitivity, and in the author's opinion most only work properly if the flashes are so close together and at such an angle as to make photography a very limited proposition.

The same applies to the many 'computer' electronic units now on the market, most of which include a built-in slave unit, or electric eye as it is sometimes called. I would thoroughly recommend that you insist on a demonstration in the store before buying any such equipment. If both flashes will not fire with the guns positioned at least 12′ apart and subtending an angle of 90° from a hypothetical camera position—don't buy.

Fig. 99. Another bounce flash shot, using a white paper roll for the background, was taken with the inexpensive Cosmic-35 camera. See also Fig. 74.

Mirrors

To vary lighting effects when using a single flash, there is no better accessory than a mirror. Have your model stand close to the mirror, looking at her own reflection. Keep the flash on the camera, or on the same axis if farther away, and make sure you can see both the model and the reflection. Focus on the model (not the reflection) and set the aperture accordingly.

This kind of portrait will delight you. First, you get a profile and a full face portrait in the same picture. Second, the lighting on the face is a combination of direct light from the flash plus the light reflected from the mirror. Third, the mirror image will have a nice twin-light effect on it. And it's all for the price of a single flash.

Don't think of flash as a purely utilitarian light. I've tried to show you that it can produce the most varied effects, and also simulate natural indoor lighting. The full-length picture at Fig. 93 was made by a combination of bounce flash and some light from a window at the rear.

The advantage of the modern electronic unit with nickel cadmium battery is that you have, once and for all, an everlasting power source and a flashtube that will not need replacing for about 10,000 flashes. The light is usually much faster than a flashbulb, too, and is balanced for use with daylight colour film.

Disadvantages of the electronic unit are: that it needs recharging after thirty or forty flashes, though the more powerful guns will give three times this number. Recharging will take anything from three to fourteen hours. The flashes themselves are cheap enough to be discounted. One type of electronic unit has either replaceable high tension batteries or replaceable nickel cadmium ones. Thus, spare charged batteries can be carried.

The simple flashbulb gun is much lighter and will stow in a camera bag with a dozen or so small flashbulbs. If the gun is not used for lengthy periods of time, the battery will go flat, and may even leak and ruin the flashgun circuits. Moral: remove the battery when not in use, and check its efficiency before going on holiday.

Know-how

Know-how is still the one accessory we cannot buy. We just have to pick it up as we go along. It isn't quite the same thing as experience, but the two often go hand-in-hand. Photographic know-how is valuable on two counts, partly because it makes us better and more efficient photographers, and partly because it saves us a great deal of money in trial and error. Here is some of the know-how I've picked up along the photographic road, and I'm pleased to be able to hand it on to you in an easily assimilated way. Let's hope it saves you some hard-earned cash.

How to choose accessory lenses and filters rationally; use of lenshoods; short-end techniques are economical for special occasions; negative and slide care; rules for picture impact; camera cases; sport; press.

Know-how

Let's start with a maxim: *Use as little equipment as you need to cope fully with the kind of work you undertake.*
Having started your outfit with a 50mm or 58mm lens, what should your second choice be? Ought you go for a lens of 85mm or 105mm focal length; or the 135mm? Perhaps one of the wide-angles would be more useful?

If your main interest is portraiture, your obvious choice will be the 85mm—105mm lens. If your main interest is scenery and interiors, then the 35mm focal length will serve you best.

To assist in lens selection, I give here a choice-aid chart. The selections indicated are the most useful and cover all conventional aspects of the kinds of work listed. The creative photographer, though, will soon find himself exploring 'non conventional' focal lengths to increase the dramatic or aesthetic appeal of his pictures. The portraitist, for example, may occasionally use a 28mm lens to push a face to the startling perspective this would give on a 16″ × 20″ print.

Similarly, in sports photography, a very wide-angle shot taken close to goal will show the whole of the action in the goal-mouth, whereas a longer lens will reach out and bring individual areas of play up close.

mirror type

f. length mm	28	35	50–58	85–105	135	200	300–400	500	1000
Advertising	D	D	A	B	E	C	D	D	E
Architecture	C	B	A	D	D	E	E	E	E
General		C	A	B	B				
Nature			C			B	A	A	A
Pictorial	C	A	D	B	B	C			
Portrait			D	A	B	C			
Press		B	A	B		C	C	C	
Record			A						
Sport		C	B	B	A	A	A	A	A
Theatrical		B	B	A	C				

Fig. 100. By posing the girl and chick against the open door of a shed in the farmyard, a dark plain background was obtained and the subject stands out with great clarity. Agfacolor film.

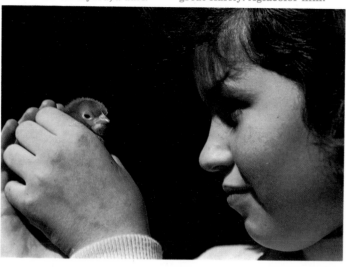

Fig. 101. A medium telephoto was used to get close to this ancient cat. High Speed Ektachrome film enabled an exposure of 1/60th at f/2.8 to be used.

Fig. 102. Just a splash of bright colour against a large subdued area is the classic formula for an eye-catching colour shot. Taken on Kodachrome film.

It has been suggested by several famous pictorial photographers that a 35mm lens plus either an 85mm, or a 135mm will cope with ninety-nine per cent of photography. The wide-angle includes the whole scene and allows you to have a strong foreground object related to the background. The longer lens brings significant detail from the scene. The camera bags of many photographers would seem to prove this, and certainly, during several years in Fleet Street I used only those two lenses ninety-five per cent of the time.

Other accessories

A mere catalogue of the effects obtained on black and white film with various colour filters leaves the photographer with the impression that he cannot make the most of his work unless he carries half-a-dozen of these attractive circles of coloured glass. Here is a reminder of the main uses of the more common filters.

UV: Only darkens skies on panchromatic film at high altitudes. Useful with colour film when the light is cold. Otherwise simply protects the lens.

Fig. 103. The soft browns of this bowl of nuts makes an attractive colour picture. Taken in sunlight near a window.

Some things are so familiar we pass them by. A closer look may reveal a worthwhile shot.

Y1:	Darkens blue skies on black and white film. Good for snow pictures in sun, as blue shadows darken.
Y2:	As Y1, but increased contrast.
O2:	Darkens skies considerably more than Y filters.
YG:	Yellow-green is preferred where much foliage is prominent. Effect on blue skies similar to Y1. Retains tanned skin tones outdoors, whereas yellow filters lighten it.
R2:	Blackens skies. Brings out grain in furniture.

The above are for black and white photography. The remainder are for colour film.

UV, haze, pink, 1a:	Removes slight blue cast caused by strong skylight or in shade.
82:	Prevents too much yellowness with early or late sun. Needs $\frac{1}{3}$ stop exposure increase.
81A:	Stronger effect than UV, makes colour pictures warm in very bluish light.

Fig. 104. Wedding shots can be informal as well as posed. Most brides want the formal groups, but are also delighted with pictures such as this. Made from a 6 × 6cm Ektachrome transparency.

Now here is a guide to the selection of filters for black and white photography. The filters for colour film are generally useful, though personally I never carry the 82. I prefer my early mornings and late evenings yellow.

	Filter and Factor					
Subject	UV	Y1	Y2	YG	O2	R2
	1	1.5	2	2	3	6
Advertising			A	C	B	
Architecture			A		B	C
General			A	B	C	
Nature			A	B		
Pictorial			A	C	B	
Portrait				A		
Press		A				
Record			A	C		B

(A blue filter darkens yellow or red on documents)

Lenshoods

The purpose of a lenshood is to prevent stray light rays entering the lens, reflecting from either lens surfaces or the interior of the camera, and causing fog and reflection marks on the film. Obviously, the protective effect of a hood is most pronounced when the light source is behind the subject. It's a good habit to keep a lenshood in place on the lens, but one should never miss a picture simply by taking time off to search out and fit a lenshood.

Short-end technique

From time to time, we all need to take just one or two pictures, perhaps a copying job or a passport picture. Developing a whole 20 or 36-exposure film with just a couple of exposures on it is too wasteful. On the other hand, time may not allow us to wait until the whole film has been exposed in the normal course of events.

The answer is to keep a few clean re-loadable cassettes

Figs. 105 & 106. Bounce flash from a powerful electronic flashgun was used to make these two pictures of teenagers dancing. Giving just enough exposure keeps the colour well saturated and helps simulate the mood.

handy. In the darkroom these can be loaded with short lengths cut from bulk film which is bought more cheaply than cassettes. Having one or two of these loaded with different kinds of black and white film, sufficient for eight or twelve exposures, means that you are always ready to undertake the odd assignment.

If you use a medium speed film for general work, you might occasionally want to take a few shots on high speed film, or even experiment with optimum recording technique on a very slow emulsion. Lengths cut from a five-metre length of HP4, Tri-X, or Agfapan 400 will take care of the fast stuff, while a length of Pan F, Panatomic-X or Agfapan 25 will take care of the records.

I don't suggest that you must use the short-end technique if you are not to miss out on important shots, but you will find it useful on occasions. Keep the re-loadable cassettes clean by blowing them out with a blower brush, and flicking any possible grit from the velvet light-trapping with the edge of a clean nailfile.

Fig. 107. Idyllic scenes like this happen on every holiday, and the photographer who keeps his eye alert will have slides to be proud of. Kodachrome film.

Fig. 108. There's no reason why beach shots should always show people looking into the lens. A little imagination, and your holiday shots will give a great deal more pleasure to the family, and prestige to you.

Negative and slide care

Nothing gets lost more quickly than a negative that hasn't been filed. It is an excellent idea to begin the way you intend to go on, so that at any time on a future occasion you will be able to find a particular negative to print from. It's surprising how often we shall be asked to make a re-print of some favourite wedding picture, holiday group or portrait. And it's very nice to be able to supply it without turning out cupboards, drawers and boxes.

The easiest filing system I know is simply to cut each film into six strips of six, and contact print these on a Paterson contact printer. The six strips of negatives are then wrapped

Fig. 109. Note how the seated figure forms a squarer shape than when standing. This allows you to fill the frame better, and gives more impact. The same applies to kneeling poses. Soft patio light, and Ektachrome film.

Fig. 110. Again, soft reflected light from the walls of a patio give superb lighting in keeping with the appeal of this delicate portrait.

in a sheet of clean paper and filed inside a $10\frac{1}{2}'' \times 4\frac{1}{2}''$ cartridge envelope. On top one writes the name of the job and a consecutive filing number. The same number is written on the back of the related contact sheet. The envelopes are filed in a shoe box or filing box, and the contact sheets punched through and kept in a stationer's file. Keep a small book with consecutive job numbers, dates, and brief descriptions. In this way, you'll be able to find negatives by job, sheet and negative numbers written on the back of original enlargements you have made, or by date or description.

There are many excellent systems for filing slides. Two of the best are slide boxes holding four 36-exposure magazines ready for projecting, and clear acetate filing sheets containing pockets for various numbers and sizes of mounted or unmounted transparencies. The former are excellent for filing made-up slides you have already sorted into magazines for projection. Every dealer has a selection of such boxes, and most are quite modestly priced. The acetate sheets with pockets are more suitable for general storage and for sorting out quantities of slides into shows, lectures, and so on. It is far easier to select from thirty-six transparencies when one can see them all at once. Among the best are those made and supplied by Diana Wyllie Limited. These are called Viewpacks, and can be supplied in filing books with slip covers for the shelf.

Impact

In *This is Photography*, Part 1, I have stressed the importance of simplicity of image. For your consideration, here is a set of 'rules' that will lead to successful pictures:

(1) Try to see the viewfinder image as a flat, two-dimensional picture, composed of various shapes and lines.
(2) A few bold masses nicely contrasting with each other are more satisfying to the eye than a confusion of small details.
(3) If it doesn't actually help the composition, eliminate it.
(4) The best way to eliminate is to get closer to the subject.

Fig. 111. Apparently unposed, this little French child was asked to look at the photographer over her burden of hot loaves. Golden crust and blonde hair, together with the diagonal line of the loaves, makes an attractive souvenir shot.

Fig. 112. This mother and child shot is full of life, because they were asked to talk. Natural affection soon turned this into an appealing picture. Kodachrome film.

Fig. 113. The yacht is probably still tethered to the quayside, but the feeling is of action. The girl has been posed so that the picture looks as though she has glanced up for a moment.

Fig. 114. Strong shapes make strong compositions. The arch makes a good frame for the scene beyond.

Fig. 115. Glamour shots should be natural looking, too. The white shirt stands out boldly against the patchy red wall, carefully chosen because of its casual appearance. The tilt of the head adds to the natural look.

115

Fig. 116. Blarney Castle in Ireland is famous, but not very pictorial. It has been made so in this shot by the inclusion of the cow in the foreground.

Fig. 117. To get correct exposure for stained glass windows, like these in the fishermen's church at Kinsale, Ireland, take a close-up reflected light reading.

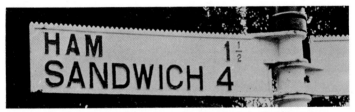

Fig. 118. Keep a good look out for humorous signposts like this, or any kind of oddity. The author once photographed the landlord of the Rainbow Inn wearing a waistcoat with a rainbow on it. It sold many times.

(5) Fill the viewfinder, and thus the final print or slide, for maximum impact.

(6) Don't be hidebound by textbooks that suggest all pictures must have a full range of tones and be pinsharp. A degree of blur often helps the feeling of movement, and harsh contrast can enhance or embolden a subject treatment.

(7) Pastel shades with a tiny brightly coloured accent can be more effective than masses of strong colour. The camera

is not as selective as the eye, which is why a bed of mixed flowers is a bad subject for colour film. See figs.87 & 88.

Camera cases

Don't make the mistake many amateurs make of buying a large case to take your whole photographic outfit. Such cases are unwieldy, and contain far more than we'll ever need on a single job. Far better to use a medium sized case that allows you to have camera and lenses ready for use with lenshoods in place. Pack this according to the kind of photography in hand. Narrow, deep cases in which equipment is packed in 'layers' are worse than useless, as equipment on top has to be removed before the gear underneath can be got at. Use a non-slip rubber pad on the shoulder strap, and carry your case so that the flap or lid opens away from you, revealing the contents more easily.

Fig. 119. This picture made at a speedway meeting was exposed at ¼ second at night, while panning. The elongated lights and general blur give the feeling of speed and excitement. Tri-X film.

Fig. 119a. A shutter speed of 1/250th second is fast enough provided the camera is panned smoothly with the moving subject.

Sport

For track events longer lenses are invariably used. In car and motorcycle racing, press photographers are often on the lookout for spills and thus tend to congregate near dicey parts of the track. The photographers who service the sports magazines, on the other hand, place themselves at favoured vantage points where good action shots of cars and bikes can be made.

A 200mm or 300mm lens may be pre-focused on a point in a bend around which motorcycles will come. The photographer watches the riders in his viewfinder screen and clicks carefully just *before* they reach the point of sharpest focus. Though they do not appear to be moving fast, due to the flattened perspective of the long viewpoint, they will have reached the point of sharp focus by the time the shutter begins to move. Waiting until they appear sharp in the viewing screen is too late.

The sports photographer needs to 'pan'. That is, he stands comfortably, holding the camera firmly against his

Fig. 120. This beautiful girl has been given a fairly small part of the frame as she crosses a bridge with springy step. Her relative size relates her to the surroundings. The low camera angle increases her importance, though not her size.

Fig. 121. During this cup presentation at a camera club, the photographer has stood on a chair and used a wide-angle lens. This relates the important foreground figures to the club members in the background. Natural light. HP4 film.

Fig. 122. Printed on a normal grade of paper, this potpourri jar would have appeared grey and uninteresting. Using high contrast enlarging paper eliminates many half tones and reveals the pattern of the subject. FP4 film.

Fig. 123. The same potpourri jar as Fig. 122, seen close up from above. Perspective is now quite evident, and the effect is entirely different.

face. As a car, or runner, approaches, he swings the camera smoothly, keeping the subject central in the viewfinder, squeezing the release button as the subject flashes past. This is far easier than it may seem, and a little practice at a roundabout near your home, at first without, then with film in the camera, will make you expert. Practise squeezing the release button until you know the precise moment at which the exposure will be made.

Fig. 124. This is the kind of meaningless pose that novices often take. The girl is obviously twisted into an unnatural and contrived position, and the general effect is poor. Compare with Fig. 125.

Fig. 125. Compare with Fig. 124. Here, the model was asked to go up on her toes at the moment of exposure, giving a shout for joy. Certainly posed, but far more effective than Fig. 124.

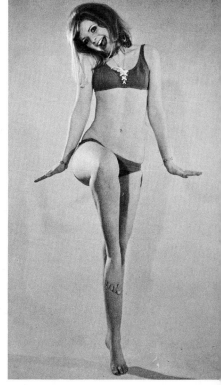

Press

Photo-journalism is perhaps the most important application in the field of visual communications, and today's press photographer has a combination of many talents. He instinctively gets himself in the right position to catch personalities when they appear at an event. He learns to handle his equipment without always looking at it. His physical reflexes are fast, and backed up by a newsman's sense of 'hunch' or 'nose for news' which tells him when something is about to happen. He is experienced enough to make snap judgements about exposure when necessary, though he will always use a meter when time allows or lighting conditions are unusual.

It is wide knowledge gained over a period of time that makes a good pressman. As time goes by he learns the tricks of the trade, odd poses, angles, or gimmicks that can produce an unusual picture from a mundane or hackneyed situation.

There is no short cut to staff press photography. Most start on a go-ahead local or provincial paper, gain experience, then decide whether the effort to reach the hurly burly and insecurity of Fleet Street is worth the candle.

Press photographers divide into two categories, though these frequently overlap. 'Press photographer' usually describes the man working for the newspapers, and aiming at a single, punchy photograph. 'Photo-journalist' is more often used to describe the magazine photographer, who uses more pictures to tell a story in greater depth.

It is a very exciting field of photography, but with the press suffering great economic cutbacks, one could hardly describe it as a job with an assured future.

Cine

A very clear-sighted photographer once described the difference between stills and movies by pointing out that the still picture captures an instant in time, whereas the movie captures a sequence in time. Good filming can produce poetry in motion, re-enacting the flight of gulls or Jumbos against the blue vault of the sky, golden hair undulating in the breeze, or the peasant spinning of timeworn hands. Good filming can re-live the sparkling moments when life is lived fully, playing, befriending, loving, enjoying. Filming can do these things but it has a technique just as any other art form, and a little study can put you on the road to mastery.

Successful movie making in eight steps: zooming—panning—tripod—shot breakdown —screen direction—matching action— editing in camera—indoor lighting.

Cine
Quarz-5

The Quarz-5 is an 8mm double-run cine camera that can do most of the things even an advanced amateur might want to do, and do them well. The specification is impressive, and even more so when you begin comparing prices. It is fitted with a Meteor–2–3 zoom lens covering the range 9mm to 36mm, with a relative aperture of f/2.4. The camera has a built-in exposure meter for semi-automatic exposure setting, five running speeds and devices for single frame exposures, continuous run and backwinding the film.

The Quarz-5 has an optical viewfinder. Magnification is from 0.5X to 2X, with 1X magnification at a focal length of 18mm, which is midway on the zooming range. Shooting length of the film on the spool is 2 × 7.5 metres. The film speed setting range is 12–100 ASA. It weighs about 3 lbs. and is supplied complete with the following accessories:

Filters: light and medium yellow, artificial-to-daylight filter for using artificial light type colour film outdoors, two neutral density filters for reducing total light flux. Two close-up lenses.

Pistol grip: giving comfortable, steady grip, and incorporating a safety wrist strap.

Extras: adapter screw for different tripod screw fittings, cable release, splitter, cleaning brush, lenshood, backwind key, rubber eyecup, caps for the lens and exposure meter window, and a rigid, fitted carrying case to take the whole outfit.

8 Points to success

Let's assume you have your cine camera loaded, wound, and ready for your first epic. Whether you intend to produce a major production or young Hubert crawling up the beach,

Fig. 126. The Quarz-5 cine camera has an f/2.4 zoom lens, with range from 9mm wide-angle to 36mm telephoto. With built-in exposure meter, five filming speeds and many professional features, it comes complete with all accessories for extremely varied filming. Film size, 8mm.

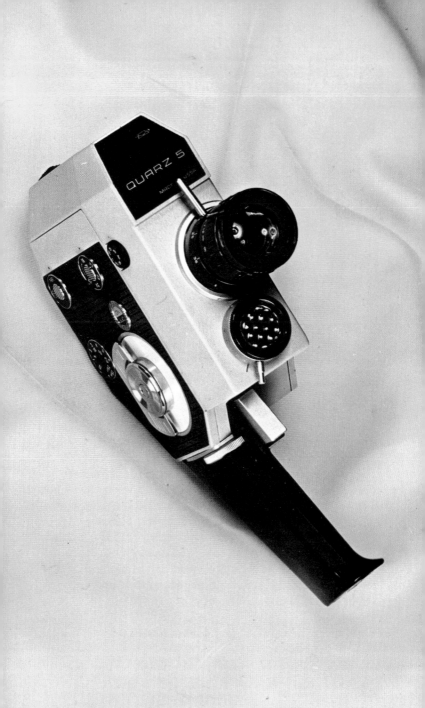

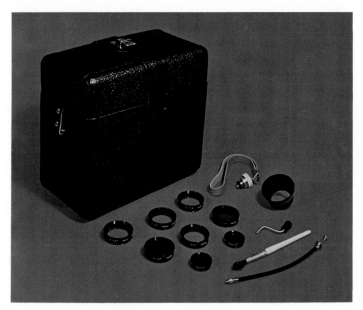

Fig. 127. The fitted case and accessories for the Quarz-5 cine camera give the amateur film maker everything, and every facility needed for even the most ambitious production.

you'll make a better job of it if you keep in mind a few simple guide lines to successful filming. Here they are:

Zooming

Don't. That's professional advice. Or, if you must, do it no more than once in every minute's filming. Nothing is more irritating to the viewer's eye than an image that keeps swelling and diminishing on the screen. Zoom only when it is actually going to improve the sequence. For example, you may be wanting to show that your female lead is sunning herself discreetly between some rocks on the beach. Every reason then to show the whole beach, then zoom in slowly to the girl. This is establishing location, then drawing attention to detail.

Panning

The smaller the film gauge the worse the effect of panning, which simply means moving the lens in a panoramic arc, usually along the horizon. To do this successfully on an

8mm cine camera means using a tripod and panning so slowly that it's hardly worth it and, in any case, uneconomical on your film stock. You'll be far better off planning each sequence and shooting it with the camera held steady. Remember the most important words in cinephotography: don't hosepipe. Keep the camera still and let the subject move. There's one kind of pan that is a great help, though, and that's the zip pan. At the end of a sequence you simply sweep the camera wildly away and stop shooting. Start your next sequence with a similar zip and you've joined two sequences without the need for editing. You can also pan up to the sky at the end of one sequence, down from the sky for the start of the next.

A good tripod

Who wants to carry a cine tripod on holiday? No one, except the chap who takes his hobby seriously and wants to turn out something more ambitious than the general run of family movies. Get in the habit of using your cine tripod properly and it is far less bother to carry around. Imagine the tripod legs erected, the point of the triangle away from you. To pick up, simply fold the back two legs together, pulling in the front one at the same time, rest the camera over your shoulder so the tripod feet are clear of the ground, and start walking. To set up, simply reverse the procedure. The dead steadiness a tripod imparts lets you—and your audience—enjoy fine quality 8mm movies.

Break down your shots

Spend five minutes with paper and ballpoint before starting your movie, and you'll have a better movie. The key word is continuity. Arrange your sequences to follow each other naturally. With a still camera you take shots as they occur—daughter, mother, cottage, son, street sign, sheep. With cine, try to make things happen in a logical sequence . . . . mother and daughter get out of car and walk over to sheep. They turn and beckon son, who comes from car. They get back in car which drives off, goes out of shot. Street sign. Family leaving car in front of old cottage . . . . think about your result and plan with variety. Long shots

alternating with medium or close-up. Long sequences
alternating with short ones. Five seconds is quite a time on
the screen, twenty a lifetime. Use cutaways—two-second
shots of spectators, faces, objects, to connect two visually
unrelated sequences.

Screen direction

This is something that needs careful attention. Johnnie is
running left to right of you in your first shot. You then
decide to move across to the other side of him. Even though
he is still running in the same direction, on the same screen,
he will appear to be returning the way he came. Note how
chases are arranged in cowboy movies. If a horse changes
direction, the camera records it before camera position is
changed. There's then a transition movement towards or
away from the camera before the change of direction is
made.

Matching action

This is directly related to screen direction. It means that
where movement takes place in one sequence then continues
in the next, there has to be a reference point so that the eye
recognises continuity of location. Imagine visitors leaving
the house via the front door. First shot is taken from the
hall looking towards the door. The next shot can be
taken from the garden path as they come through the door.

If a head is turned back towards the camera in the first
shot, it should be turned away from the camera at the start
of the second.

Editing in camera

A great deal of editing can be done while you shoot,
saving a lot of time cutting and splicing later. Even if you
love cutting and splicing, camera editing is good, tight
technique that produces good, tight movies. We've already
described zip pans and sky shots, as well as cutaways.
Another useful technique is the 'walk-on, walk-off' sequence,
which is also an excellent way of matching action. Suppose
a boy and girl, hand in hand, are running towards the
camera. Arrange for the girl to run her tummy right on to
the lens, and stop. You stop shooting as tummy touches

lens. With the couple standing still, you walk round behind them, and put the lens in the middle of the girl's back. Start the camera, then immediately order the couple to continue running. In the film you'll have made a splendid blackout transition from one sequence to the next. You can also finish a sequence by zooming in to a white patch, say a dress, then zooming back from another white object to start the next sequence. Or, using a tripod, you can fade out by closing down the aperture, or fade in by opening it.

Indoor lighting

Cine lights, consisting of a quartz iodine lamp or a pair of photoflood lamps on a bar to which the camera is attached, bears the same relation to cine photography as flash-on-camera bears to stills. It is a strictly utilitarian light. The action and people may look great, but the light looks ghastly. To make a really good job of cine lighting indoors

Fig. 128. The Russ Dual Gauge cine projector is the companion to the Quarz-5 cine camera, and has just as professional a specification. It takes single and double-run 8mm, and Super 8, is built to the highest mechanical and optical standards, and will synchronise with a tape recorder.

you would need three reflector photofloods and one reflector photospot (lamps incorporating their own silvered reflector), with stands or clamps. An excellent compromise, bright enough for shooting colour, is to use two 1000w. quartz iodine lamps, one aimed at the ceiling, the other at the wall nearest to your subject. Though bright, this will not cause people to screw up their eyes, as often happens with direct lighting.

Those are my eight points for success, and I do commend

Fig. 129. Technotank single allows the amateur to process a 30′ length of 8mm or 16mm cine film at home. After loading, further operations can be carried out by daylight.

them to your attention before you go off to shoot your movies. The results will be far more satisfying.

Projection

A fitting companion for the Quarz-5 cine camera is the Russ Dual Projector. This is a precision machine, smooth and quiet in operation, that will handle Single 8, Super 8, and Standard 8 films. It has an 18mm f/1.4 lens and this, together with the dichroic reflector and 100w. tungsten halogen lamp, produces a brilliant screen image with very

Fig. 130. This is the Technotank Double, which allows two 30′ lengths of film to be processed at the same time. Solutions are introduced and emptied by means of tubes.

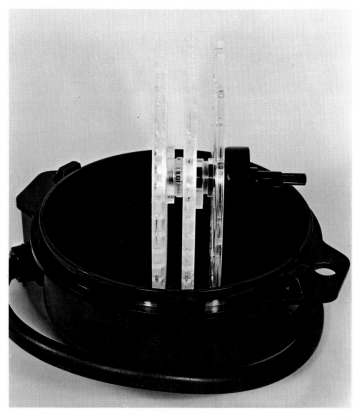

little gate heat. A near-professional specification includes preliminary filament heating for long lamp life, two-level light output, forward, reverse and still projection, plus power rewind. Projection speed is infinitely variable between 12 and 26 frames per second, and there is provision for synchronisation of tape recordings. The Russ Dual Projector is supplied complete with A1/215 lamp, three 400′ take-up reels, comprehensive accessory kit and large fitted holdall case.

A useful extra is the tape synchroniser which couples to the take-up spool of almost any reel-to-reel tape recorder. It will give synchronisation of commentary and/or background music, with the projector running at 16 frames per second. The unit, which is of diecast alloy construction, has a neon strobe speed adjuster, and is suitable for any of the previous Luch projectors or the new Russ Dual.

Home processing

For the real enthusiast who wants to process his own film, there is the beautifully made Technotank. This will take 30′ of 8mm or 16mm film on its clear plastic spiral, and once loaded, processing can be carried out in daylight. Solution changing is by inlet and outlet pipes. A simple and efficient film splitter is supplied to cut double-run 8mm film down the centre. A double tank will take two lengths of film at one load.

Binoculars
& Microscopes

Have you ever thought how the world of
ordinary vision extends from about three feet
to fifteen feet or thereabouts? Walk along the
street or woodland path and most of the
things you'll notice will be within that
distance—psychologically, this is the distance
you can be affected from! Occasionally, we
strain our vision to scrutinise the gay shell of
the ladybird, or the Middle World vision of
sun-capped peaks, but we live and see
mainly in what the film director calls
'medium shot'. There are worlds of
fascination, near and far, that we can never
know with the unaided eye. Looking
through a good binocular for the first time
can be a delightful shock as you suddenly
encompass the whole wide world, like
driving afield in your first car. At the other
end of the scale, I remember the powerful
sense of life when my cousin, a doctor,
showed me coloured spheres in a jerky ballet
under the microscope. Binos and micros
extend your vision, and I think you also see
better with the unaided eye afterwards.
Binoculars teach the photographer all about
telephoto lenses, as they fold up the
landscape into all sorts of pictorial
possibilities.

Binoculars and how to choose them; what
the jargon means; microscope photography
with the single-lens reflex.

Binoculars & Microscopes

Some binoculars are fine for pastimes like girl-watching, while others are ideal for spotting a poacher at two miles. If your hobbies are wide and largely based on your photography, you'll be best suited by a pair of 7 × 50 glasses, but before telling you which pair of binoculars is best for a particular job, let's sort out the terminology used in describing binos. It's only confusing if you don't understand it.

Start with the designation we are all familiar with— 8 × 30, 7 × 50, etcetera. Most people are vaguely aware that the first number has something to do with the magnification, but they are hazy about the 30 or the 50. Yes, the first number is simply the degree of magnification or, if you prefer, the number of times larger the object will look than with the unaided eye. The second number, the 30 or 50, or whatever, describes the diameter of the objective, or front lens, as measured in millimetres. The greater the diameter of the front lens in relation to the degree of magnification, the brighter the vision will be. Binoculars with wide front lenses are often called 'night glasses',

Fig. 131. Lightweight 6 × 24 binoculars are a good choice for general and theatre viewing, though more powerful than the so-called theatre glass. All Russian binoculars are built to the highest precision and are optically superb.

Fig. 132. The 7 × 50 glass is a favourite for yachting, general observation, and night viewing.

Fig. 133. The 8 × 30 binocular is
an excellent day glass for sport,
spotting, and general work.

Fig. 134. The powerful 12 × 40
binocular is the choice of bird-
watchers and those who insist
on knowing the colour of the
captain's eyes as well as the
name of his ship.

because they have more light-gathering capability.

Another impressive term is 'exit pupil', which describes the diameter of the ray of light that reaches your eye via the eyepiece. It is determined by dividing the diameter of the objective lens by the power of magnification. Thus, a 7×50 binocular has a large exit pupil of 7.1mm, while an 8×30 has an exit pupil only 3.8mm. The 7×50 will, therefore, give a far brighter view, though the magnification is not quite as great.

The field of view of a binocular is stated as X number of feet at 1000 yards. A binocular is often engraved with a Field number, such as Field 7.5°. A degree equal 52.5' at 1000 yards, so Field 11.0° means that a particular binocular will cover a field of 577.5' at that distance.

There are many cheap binoculars on the market and some are quite good. The advantage of a real quality binocular, though, is its complete freedom from faults such as colour fringing, and the superior definition of the image. Here are a representative selection from the various powers available:

A lightweight 6×24 ideal for theatre and general viewing, an 8×30 for sports, spotting and general work with more magnification, a 7×50 for yachting, general observation and night viewing, and a very powerful 12×40 for bird-watching and similar occupations. It should be borne in mind that the greater the magnification the harder it is to obtain a steady image unless the binocular can be rested against something.

Model	12×40	7×50	8×30	6×24
Magnification	12X	7X	8X	6X
Angular field of view	6°	6°48'	8°30'	11°30'
Front lens diameter	40mm	50mm	30mm	24mm
Exit pupil diameter	3.3mm	7.1mm	3.8mm	4.0mm
Resolving power in seconds of arc	5	6	7.5	9
Weight, gms.	850	980	660	530

At the other end of the scale we have the wonder world of microscopy, available to the single-lens reflex user by means of a microscope adapter. When fitted, and with the subject suitably illuminated, subjects can be photographed at magnifications well beyond 1000X. This is really a world that needs exploring. Invisible even with the use of bellows and extension tubes, it becomes an awe-inspiring experience at 200X, 400X or 600X magnification. Tiny cells jostle each other and bustle along like human beings in the street, tiny scraps of paper, coal, bone, clay, water, give an insight into the very texture of the world we live in—nay, the world we are composed of. And what a beautiful world it is! A microscopic world with its own microscopic sunsets and oceans and storms—all in a drop of fluid.

The least expensive and most suitable instrument for use in photomicrography of the Russian range of microscopes is the model MBR-1E, which has coarse and fine adjustment (graduated in 0.002mm divisions). The microscope also has a rack and pinion focusing substage and Abbé condenser (aperture 1.2), quadruple nosepiece, achromatic objectives 8X, 20X, and 40X, inclined monocular tube and 7X, 10X, and 15X, huyghenian eyepieces. This instrument has a range of total magnifications of 56X to 600X and both lower and higher power objectives can be fitted. Suitable high intensity lamps can also be provided giving Kohler illumination which is essential for first-class results. Various types of vertical tubes are available to accommodate single-lens reflex cameras. In addition to normal bright field photomicrography, other effects can be obtained by using

Fig. 135. Medical slides have meaning for doctors, but are fascinating colour patterns to the lay microscope user.

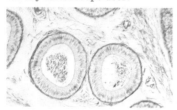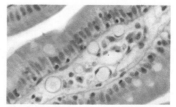

138

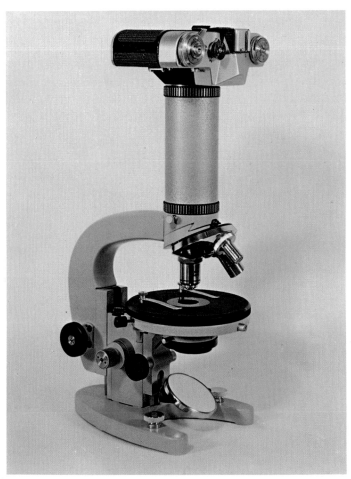

Fig. 136. Russian high-power MBR microscope, with Zenith camera attached, can explore the wonderworld of micro- photography, as well as providing valuable scientific and clinical information.

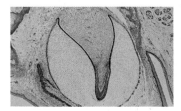

polarised light, and dark field illumination which shows the specimen brilliantly illuminated against a black background.

Full descriptions of Russian microscopes ranging from the most simple instrument model SHM-1 to the research microscope model MBB-1A can be had on request from the Microscope Division, Technical & Optical Equipment (London) Limited.

The Company

Technical & Optical Equipment was formed in 1962 with the object of marketing Russian photographic and microscope equipment. Right at the beginning, two major factors were put at the forefront of Company policy. First, the public must be offered a value-for-money product. Second, and equally important, that product must be backed up by the finest and most reliable pre-sales and after-sales service. This became the Company's watchword and consequently, when the Company moved into its first offices in Earlham Street, London, the first department to be fully equipped was the Workshop.

It was necessary to build up distribution through the established photographic dealers and it is a well-known fact that any product that is to be stocked and promoted successfully by the dealer must be backed by an adequate stock of spares, plus a fast turn-round on Service. The proof of the success of Technical & Optical Equipment's early policy became apparent when, after only two years of trading, it was necessary to move from their original offices to much larger premises in St. Martin's Lane, London.

By this time, a rapidly growing number of dealers were acknowledging the value for money offered by the early reflex and rangefinder cameras, and were stocking these items in greater quantity all the time. The constantly swelling volume of business has necessitated two further moves, one to Praed Street, and now to the impressive new building, Zenith House in London, N.7., designed specifically for Technical & Optical Equipment's function. The internal layout of Zenith House is divided into specific functional sections which embrace Sales and Marketing, Service and Inspection, Accounts, Sales Administration, Stores and Despatch.

The Company regularly organises photographic competitions for users of Russian cameras, with prizes and trips arranged for the winners. The huge response in terms of entries is an indication of the enthusiasm of photographers for Russian products. Not only at the amateur level, but among professionals, too, there is appreciation of the high

Fig. 137. Repair facilities at Zenith House are second to none. The latest equipment is installed and operated by highly skilled personnel. No item is released to the customer until double checked.

Fig. 138. Zenith cameras undergoing part of their rigorous check before being passed into stock. Russian cameras' reputation for reliability is well earned.

Fig. 139. Built-in exposure
meters are tested to close
tolerances on this meter
testing unit before being passed
for issue.

quality of the cameras themselves, the accessory lenses and other equipment, at prices that make them a viable proposition for the self-financing photographer. Similar competitions have been organised for dealers stocking the Company's products, and received with equal enthusiasm.

The Company's motto is, and always has been 'Priority Service', and attention is constantly given to this aspect of the Company's affairs. It gives great satisfaction to all levels of staff at Technical & Optical Equipment that 'Priority Service' is not only done, but is always seen to be done, by public and dealers alike.

Design improvements have flowed constantly from the drawing boards of designers at the home factories of Russian cameras since the Company began trading, and this has resulted in the Company being able to offer up-to-the-minute equipment. Mechanically, Russian equipment is built to the same functional and hard-wearing requirements that got the Russian space programme off the ground. The lenses themselves have improved constantly, and enjoy an enviable reputation among discerning users. Such items as the catadioptric MTO500A and MTO1000A lenses have a world-wide reputation for superior performance at an economic price.

Both reflex and rangefinder cameras are well known for efficient and reliable functioning over long periods of time, partly due to the rigid inspection given to each item before being put into stock at Zenith House.

Russian microscope equipment, it might be said, established its own reputation in a short space of time in the United Kingdom. Made to the very highest specification, and with superior design factors and finish, these microscopes are aiding medicine, science, industry and research in schools, hospitals, workshops and universities everywhere. The same priority service attaches to these instruments as to Russian cameras, with which they are often used for micro-photography.

It is Technical & Optical's proudest achievement that they offer the finest service in the photographic trade. All apparatus received from Russia is carefully inspected and

Fig. 140. The visitor to Zenith House is welcomed at reception in this fine showroom. Tastefully furnished, it contains a display of Russian equipment which the visitor may examine while waiting.

packed before despatch to ensure that the dealer receives the equipment not only in pristine condition, but in perfect working order ready for sale.

Some dealers make a point in their advertising that all equipment received from importers of even the world's most expensive cameras is checked in their own workshop, and that a high percentage of such cameras need adjustment before being passed on to the customer. This is seldom the case with Russian equipment, and the dealer who informs Technical & Optical that an item has reached him in less than perfect order is indeed becoming a rarity.

The confidence thus engendered in dealers, and consequently among the public, is rewarded by the continuously-growing sales of the whole range of Russian photographic and microscope equipment.

Useful Charts

Lens Specifications

LENS	FOCAL LENGTH	CONSTRUCTION	ANGLE OF VIEW	DISTANCE SCALE	DIAPHRAGM
ORION 15	28mm	4 elements in 4 groups	75°	1m – INF.	Manual f/6-22
JUPITER 12	35mm	6 elements in 4 groups	63°	1m – INF.	Manual f/2.8-22
MIR 1	37mm	6 elements in 3 groups	60°	0.7m – INF.	Manual pre-set f/2.8-16
INDUSTAR 50	50mm	4 elements in 3 groups	45°	0.65m – INF.	Manual f/3.5 – 16
JUPITER 8	50mm	6 elements in 3 groups	45°	1m – INF.	Manual f/2 – 22
INDUSTAR 61	52mm	4 elements in 3 groups	45°	1m – INF.	Manual f/2.8 – 16
HELIOS 44	58mm	6 elements in 4 groups	40°	0.5m – INF.	Manual pre-set f/2 – 16
MIR 3	65mm	6 elements in 5 groups	66°	0.8m – INF.	Semi-Auto pre-set f/3.5 – 22
INDUSTAR 29	80mm	4 elements in 3 groups	53°	0.9m – INF.	Semi-auto pre-set f/2.8 – 22
JUPITER 9	85mm	7 elements in 3 groups	28°	0.8m – INF.	Manual pre-set f/2 – 16
JUPITER 9	85mm	7 elements in 3 groups	28°	1.15m – INF.	Manual f/2 – 22
JUPITER 11	135mm	4 elements in 3 groups	18°30'	1.4m – INF.	Manual pre-set f/4 – 16
JUPITER 11	135mm	4 elements in 3 groups	18°30'	2.5m – INF.	Manual f/4 - 22
TELEMAR 22	200mm	4 elements in 3 groups	12°30'	2.5m – INF.	Manual pre-set f/5.6 – 22
TAIR 3A	300mm	3 elements in 3 groups	8°	2.2m – INF.	Manual pre-set f/4.5 – 22
TAIR 33	300mm	4 elements in 3 groups	15°	3m – INF.	Manual pre-set f/4.5 – 22
MTO 500A	550mm	Catadioptric system – 4 elements in 3 groups	5°	4m – INF.	Fixed at f/8.5
MTO 1000A	1100mm	Catadioptric system – 5 elements in 3 groups	2.5°	10m – INF.	Fixed at f/10.5

FILTER SIZE	LENGTH	WEIGHT	FITTING
40.5mm Thread or 51mm Push-On	32mm approx.	80g approx.	Fed/Zorki
40.5mm Thread or 51mm Push-On	58mm approx.	130g approx.	Fed/Zorki
49mm Thread or 51mm Push-On	57mm approx.	200g approx.	Zenith E/B
33mm Thread 36mm Push-On	26.5mm approx.	75g approx.	Zenith E/B
40.5mm Thread 42mm Push-On	45mm approx.	130g approx.	Zorki
40.5mm Thread 42mm Push-On	40mm approx.	140g approx.	Fed
49mm Thread 51mm Push-On	57mm approx.	220g approx.	Zenith E/B
88mm Screw	115mm approx.	620g approx.	Zenith 80
40.5mm (in Hood) or 58mm Thread	70mm approx.	340g approx.	Zenith 80
49mm Thread 51mm Push-On	67mm approx.	350g approx.	Zenith E/B
49mm Thread 51mm Push-On	80mm approx.	335g approx.	Fed/Zorki
40.5mm Thread 42mm Push-On	84mm approx.	360g approx.	Zenith E/B
40.5mm Thread 42mm Push-On	105mm approx.	360g approx.	Fed/Zorki
49mm Thread 51mm Push-On	130mm approx.	475g approx.	Zenith E/B
77mm Thread	260mm approx.	1,200g approx.	Zenith E/B
88mm Thread	246mm approx.	1,700g approx.	Zenith 80
77mm Thread	175mm approx.	1,250g approx.	Zenith E/B
120mm Thread	278mm approx.	3,200g approx.	Zenith E/B

Recommended temperature 20°C. (68°F.) G 0.55 with five seconds
agitation initially and at minute intervals.

KODAK	full-strength	1:1	1:3
Tri-X 35mm & 120	8	11	16
Tri-X Professional 120	8	10	15
Plus-X 35mm & 120 Plus-X Professional	6	8	12
Pan-X 35mm & 120, Verichrome Pan	7	9	13
Sheet Films:			
Panchro-Royal	10	—	—
Plus-X Pan	8	—	—
Tri-X Pan, Tri-X Ortho	9	—	—
Commercial Fine Grain	6	—	—
ILFORD			
HP4 35mm	$7\frac{1}{2}$	11	N.R.
HP4 120	9	$13\frac{1}{2}$	N.R.
HP3 35mm	$8\frac{1}{2}$	$12\frac{1}{2}$	N.R.
HP3 120	10	15	N.R.
FP4 35mm & 120	9	$13\frac{1}{2}$	18
Selopan	10	15	N.R.
Mark 5	7	$10\frac{1}{2}$	N.R.
Pan F	$6\frac{1}{2}$	$9\frac{1}{2}$	13
Sheet Films:			
HP3	9	—	—
HP4	8	—	—
FP4	6	—	—
AGFA			
Agfapan 25 35mm & 120	8	12	16
Isopan IF 35mm & 120	$7\frac{1}{2}$	11	15
Agfapan 100 & ISS 35mm & 120	6	9	12
Agfapan 400/1000/Ultra 35mm & 120	8	12	N.R.
Sheet Films: As for above Agfa films of the same ASA ratings.			

	Reproduction Ratio	Extension Tube Nos.	Distance Scale Setting (m)	Subject to Camera Back (mm)	Subject to Camera Back (in.)	Exposure Factor
Industar-61 (Fed 3L & 4L)	1:10.5	1	∞	655	25.8	1.1
	1:10	1	10	636	25.0	1.2
	1:10.5	1	3.5	584	23.0	1.2
	1:8	1	1.7	532	21.0	1.2
	1:7	1	1.2	481	19.0	1.3
	1:6	2	4	430	17.0	1.3
	1:5	2	1.2	379	14.9	1.4
	1:4	1+2	20	329	13.0	1.6
	1:3	3	1.8	281	11.1	1.8
	1:2	4	10	238	9.4	2.2
	1:1	2+3+4	1.2	211	8.3	4.0
	1.1:1	1+2+3+4	1	212	8.3	4.4
Jupiter-8 (Zorki-4)	1:10.5	1	∞	670	26.6	1.1
	1:10	1	10	641	25.3	1.2
	1:9	1	3.5	590	23.25	1.2
	1:8	1	1.7	538	21.2	1.2
	1:7	1	1.2	486	19.2	1.3
	1:6	2	4	435	17.2	1.3
	1:5	2	1.2	385	15.2	1.4
	1:4	1+2	20	335	13.2	1.6
	1:3	3	1.8	287	11.3	1.8
	1:2	4	4	243	9.6	2.2
	1:1	2+3+4	1.2	217	8.6	4.0
	1.1:1	1+2+3+4	1	218	8.6	4.4

Actual extension of each tube

Tube No.	mm.	in.
1	5	0.197
2	8	0.315
3	16	0.630
4	26	1.025

Technical & Optical Equipment reserve the right to alter or amend the specifications of any equipment described in this book, if and when this becomes necessary.

Price
£2·00